NIGER
in Pictures

Alison Behnke

Twenty-First Century Books

Contents

Website address: www.lernerbooks.com

Twenty-First Century Books
A division of Lerner Publishing Group, Inc.
241 First Avenue North
Minneapolis, MN 55401 U.S.A.

web enhanced @ www.vgsbooks.com

Library of Congress Cataloging-in-Publication Data

Behnke, Alison.
    Niger in pictures / by Alison Behnke.
      p. cm. — (Visual geography series)
    Includes bibliographical references and index.
    ISBN: 978-0-8225-7147-6 (lib. bdg. : alk. paper)
      1. Niger—Pictorial works—Juvenile literature. 2. Niger—Juvenile literature. I. Title.
DT547.24.B44 2008
966.26—dc22   2007025332

Manufactured in the United States of America
1 2 3 4 5 6 - PA - 13 12 11 10 09 08

INTRODUCTION

From its harsh landscape to its complex history, the Republic of Niger is a nation of contrast. Vast deserts dominate most of this landlocked nation in western Africa, creating a rugged beauty. In stark contrast to this dry expanse is the green and fertile land surrounding the Niger River. The nation takes its name from this river, which is a precious source of life and water in the arid country.

Niger's history and its character as a country are also full of contrasts. For instance, the fiercely independent Tuareg—a traditionally nomadic group of livestock herders—are very different from the politically powerful Djerma and Songhai peoples. Dozens of other ethnic groups and subgroups populate the nation with a vast variety of traditions.

Similarly, ancient Niger was not a single or unified nation. Instead, a variety of kingdoms and other realms ruled the area, often battling each other for control. Many shared an interest in trade, however, which linked the nation to distant lands. More than one thousand years ago, caravans of hundreds of camels trekked across Niger's

deserts, carrying goods between the Mediterranean Sea to the north and rich sub-Saharan empires.

These caravans also brought ideas, and beginning in the 1200s Nigerien peoples started to adopt the religion of Islam and its rich traditions. But many people blended the new religion with their ancient local faiths, resulting in a tapestry of beliefs.

Yet another new influence entered the nation in the 1920s, when Niger became a colony of France. The European nation brought new contrasts, pushing local peoples to change their lifestyles, clothing styles, and even languages. Niger's people endured French rule for close to forty years. Outside powers drew borders that had never before existed, carving up historic regions and dividing ethnic groups. While Niger's time as a French colony was fairly short compared to its long history, colonial rule left a permanent mark on the nation. Following independence in 1960, Niger experienced a long series of coups (sudden seizures of power) and political unrest.

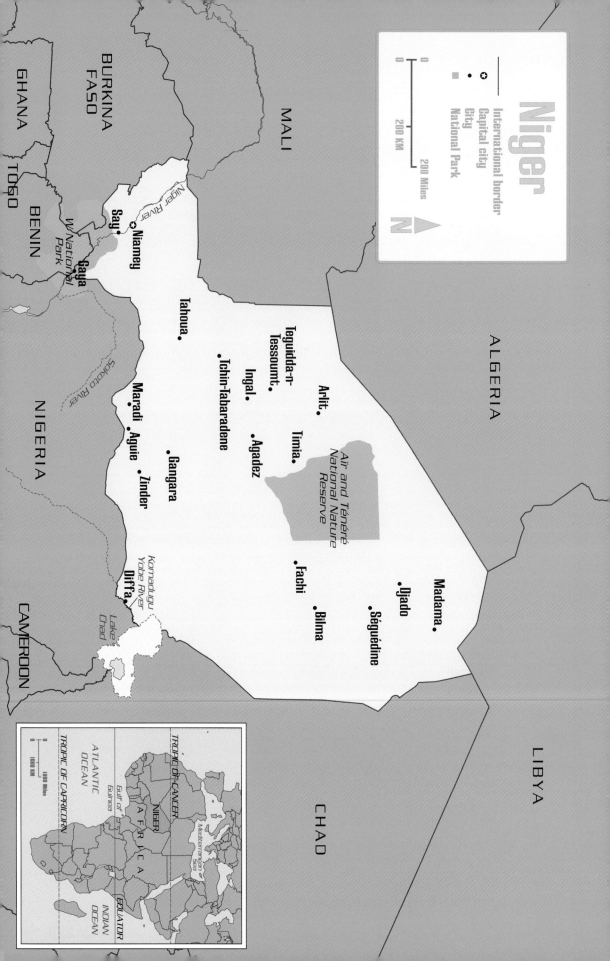

The **Réserve Naturelle Nationale de l'Aïr et du Ténéré** (Aïr and Ténéré National Nature Reserve) is the largest protected natural area in Africa.

Years of military rule, government corruption, limited democracy, and little freedom followed.

Modern Niger has moved toward a democratic government. Its culture brings together many influences in a rich mixture, blending new and old religions, traditional and modern art forms, and very different cultures. Its 14.4 million people speak many languages and follow many customs.

But many challenges still face the people of Niger, and the road ahead remains rocky. The contrasts that enrich Niger also have the potential to divide it. The country is ranked among the poorest in the world. Niger's leaders and its citizens must deal with a range of difficult problems as they try to provide a good life for themselves and their neighbors. To succeed, the nation may need to both draw upon and reconcile its many fascinating contrasts.

THE LAND

Located in northwestern Africa, the Republic of Niger has an area of 489,189 square miles (1,266,994 square kilometers). This area makes it the sixth-largest nation in Africa and almost three times the size of the U.S. state of California. Landlocked Niger shares its borders with seven neighbors. Algeria and Libya lie to the north, while Chad is located to Niger's east. Nigeria makes up most of the nation's southern boundary, but Niger also shares shorter stretches of its southern border with Benin and Burkina Faso. Mali lies to Niger's west.

Topography

Niger's landscape is made up of four primary topographical regions. These areas are the nation's deserts, the peaks of the north central Aïr Massif (Aïr Mountains), lower-altitude plateaus, and the southwestern river basin surrounding the Niger River.

By far the most dominant feature of Niger's terrain is its vast stretches of desert. In all, about four-fifths of the nation's land is desert.

Niger's northern reaches are part of the enormous Sahara, which dominates much of northern Africa. The Ténéré Desert in northeastern Niger is a smaller desert within the Sahara. The Ténéré covers more than 150,000 square miles (388,498 sq. km), some of which Niger shares with its neighbors Algeria and Chad. Though its heat is extreme and can be dangerous, the Ténéré is also considered one of the world's most beautiful deserts. Part of its unique beauty comes from a desert feature known as *ergs*. These shifting seas of sand are named for an Arabic word translated as "dune field" or "ocean." Trade winds sweep through the ergs from the northeast toward the equator, blowing the sand into migrating dunes and ever-changing crests and waves. Ergs support little to no vegetation, meaning almost no plants grow there. The region receives at most 5 to 6 inches (13 to 15 centimeters) of rain each year. Niger's deserts include several ergs, such as the Erg du Ténéré, the Great Bilma Erg, and the Jadal and Brousset ergs. In addition, the Ténéré contains a type of landform called a *reg*—a broad, flat, and stony desert plain.

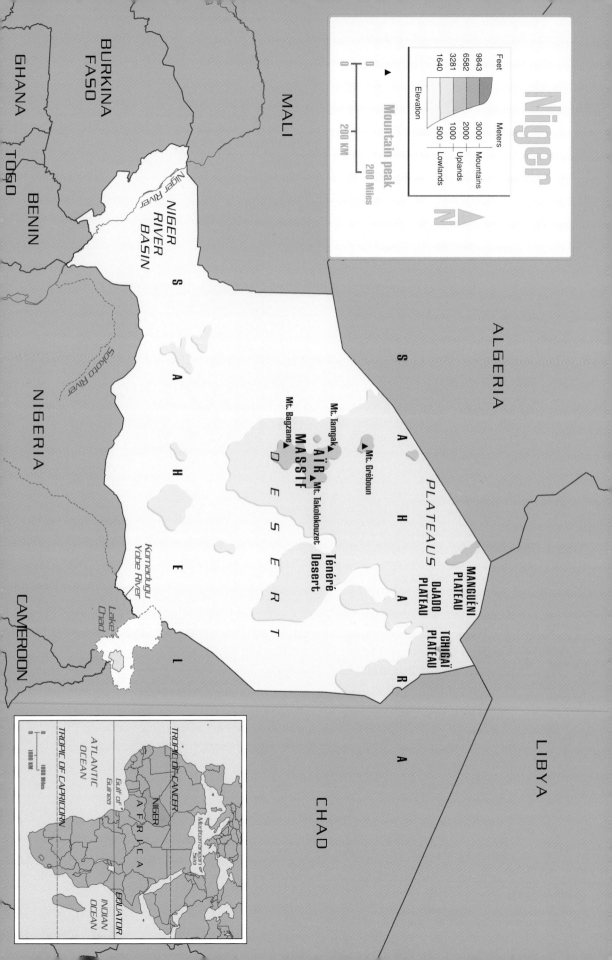

The Aïr Massif rises above **Timia,** a Tuareg town. Timia lies near an oasis, where the mountain valleys collect enough water to sustain orchards.

Within Niger's deserts lies another major topographical feature—the Aïr Massif. Lying in north central Niger, this dense group of mountains runs in ranges from north to south. It covers an area of more than 23,000 square miles (59,570 sq. km)—a little larger than the U.S. state of West Virginia. Most of the Aïr's peaks are steep and jagged. They are made of dark gray rock—much of it with volcanic origins. They rise to heights of well over 6,000 feet (1,829 meters) above sea level. Most sources list the massif's highest point—and the nation's—as Mount Bagzane, at 6,634 feet (2,022 m). Some observers claim that the highest peak is actually Mount Gréboun, but they can't agree on the mountain's height. Estimates range between 6,378 feet (1,944 m) and 7,579 feet (2,310 m). Other prominent peaks of the Aïr are Mount Tamgak and Mount Takolokouzet. Cutting between the mountains of the massif are deep valleys that locals call *koris*. Hot springs also nestle among the massif's peaks.

High plateaus make up another aspect of Niger's topography. The Djado Plateau lies northeast of the Aïr Massif, within the Ténéré Desert. It reaches altitudes of more than 1,900 feet (579 m) above sea level. To its east is the Manguéni Plateau. Even farther east is the Tchigaï Plateau, which straddles the border with Chad. Additional plateaus stretch across southern Niger in a belt about 900 miles (1,448 km) wide.

Finally, the river valley of the southwest is the nation's most hospitable area. As a result, it is home to most of Niger's people. The nation's landscape slopes down toward the Niger River from the eastern plateaus and mountains. Savannas (drought-resistant grasslands) mark the edge of the basin, which has the country's lowest average altitude. The land around the Niger River is also the nation's most fertile.

Rivers and Lakes

In a landlocked nation made up mostly of arid desert, any sources of freshwater are especially precious. The Niger River gives the country of Niger its name and also serves as its lifeblood. The third-largest river in all of Africa, it travels a total of about 2,600 miles (4,184 km). About 350 miles (563 km) of its length lies within Niger itself, running in a northwest-to-southeast direction through Niger's southwestern arm. The origins of the river's name are unclear. Some scholars believe that it comes from *negro*, the Portuguese word for "black." Others suggest that it comes from *gher n-gheren*, a phrase meaning "river among rivers" in the Tamashek language spoken by Tuareg people.

Niger was not always so dry. Evidence of ancient waterways is etched into the earth, showing courses that once flowed into the Niger and Sokoto rivers. The dried tributaries that used to flow into the Niger are called *dallol*, while those that once entered the Sokoto are called *gulbi*.

The Komadugu Yobe River forms the border between Niger and Nigeria for about 185 miles (298 km). The Komadugu Yobe drains into shallow Lake Chad, which lies across the country from the Niger River. Only a small corner of Lake Chad lies within the southeastern border of Niger (most of the lake lies in the nation of Chad), and even that section has been reduced to a marshy lakebed. In the past several decades, Lake Chad has shrunk dramatically, due to droughts (periods of severely low rainfall) and to human use of the lake's waters for irrigation and other purposes. Some people also point to the effects of global warming. Whole sections of the lake have dried up completely. Once among the largest lakes in Africa, it is just 4 percent of the area it was in the 1960s. While this dramatic reduction in water is alarming, it is not the first time it has happened. In fact, the lake's size has fluctuated with climate and precipitation (rain and snowfall) changes for thousands of years. Scientists believe that it may have dried up completely or almost completely ten times or more in the past one thousand years. They predict that this may happen again sometime in the 2000s.

The **Niger River** flows through a wide, shallow region known as a delta. This river's steady water supply feeds Niger's best farmland and biggest cities.

Other lakes in Niger are seasonal, often drying up completely during the driest part of the year. Wadis are another type of seasonal water source in Niger. These waterways flow through valleys and ravines only during the rainy season, especially running down from the Aïr Massif. Once the rains stop, the wadis usually dry out. Even the Komadugu Yobe River often dries up during the most arid months.

Most towns of any size outside of Niger's southwest are built around oases, isolated water sources in the desert. For example, the northwestern towns of Bilma and Fachi are oasis settlements.

Climate

Niger contains two major climatic bands. These regions are the vast deserts of the north and the more humid Sahel to the south. Because Niger is mostly desert and located close to the equator, it is one of the globe's hottest nations. Around the entire country and throughout the year, the average temperature is about 84°F (29°C). The hottest months are generally April and May, while the coolest months are November, December, and January. The year also has both a rainy and a dry season. The rains fall primarily from May through October, peaking in July and August. The rest of the year is extremely dry. This distinction between the rainy and dry seasons is most marked in the south and southwest, however. Niger's deserts remain mostly rainless all year round. Periodic droughts lower precipitation even more.

In the desert zone, average temperatures skyrocket above the nation's norms. In the Ténéré Desert, highs of more than 100°F (38°C) are common, and temperatures above 115°F (46°C) have been recorded. In addition, the desert goes through drastic temperature swings. Overnight lows can dip to freezing (32°F or 0°C) in the coolest months. Along with these grueling temperatures, the deserts receive very little precipitation. In many years, no more than 1 inch (2.5 cm) of rain falls. And that tiny amount of moisture may evaporate in the extreme heat even before it can reach the ground. The Aïr Massif is an exception to the rule. While it lies in the middle of the desert, it receives more precipitation than its surroundings. Up to 10 inches (25 cm) water the mountains annually, compared to the nearby town of Agadez's average yearly rainfall of 6.5 inches (16.5 cm).

The Sahel zone occupies the remainder of Niger's territory, beginning just north of the city of Tahoua. This transitional region lies between the Sahara and the more humid savannas farther to the south. Rainfall within the Sahel increases as one moves farther south. In the northern portion of the zone, rainfall is largely limited to intense, short-lived thunderstorms. Sandstorms often occur as well. Farther southwest, the area around the Niger River receives more rainfall. Niger's capital city, Niamey, lies within this region. Its average high temperatures range between 90°F and 105°F (32°C and 41°C), with lows between 60°F and 85°F (16°C and 29°C). Niamey receives an average of 22 inches (56 cm) of rain each year, and the rainy season brings uncomfortably high humidity.

The smallest and rainiest portion of southwestern Niger contains savannas. These broad, flat grasslands have few trees. Gaya, located on the Niger River in the nation's southernmost tip, receives an average of 34 inches (86 cm) each year.

I EAT DINOSAURS FOR BREAKFAST

The dramatic Ténéré Desert was not always a desert—and it was once home to enormous animals. In the early 2000s, scientists in Niger found the fossilized bones of a massive crocodile-like creature. The scientists believe that, in life, the animal was 40 feet (12 m) long and weighed 16,000 pounds (7,257 kilograms) or more. They also think that its diet included dinosaurs that lived in the region during the same era, about 110 million years ago.

A visitor leaves the **Tree of Ténéré** in the early 1970s. The tree's roots drew water from a source too deep for animals to reach.

A Rare Landmark

For decades, Niger's most famous plant was L'Arbre du Ténéré, or the Tree of Ténéré. This acacia tree was located in the middle of the Ténéré Desert, with a deep root system drawing on water far below the ground. As the only tree for about 250 miles (402 km) in any direction, it was a dramatic sight on the horizon. The tree gained legendary status, and many people regarded it as sacred. But in 1973, a driver crashed his car into the tree, snapping its trunk. The remains of the tree were moved to Niamey's National Museum, and a metal sculpture marks the tree's original desert site.

Flora and Fauna

Most of northern Niger's climate and landscape are too harsh for plants and animals to thrive or even survive. Desert vegetation, for instance, is largely limited to a few tough, spiky grasses and herbs. The acacia, a small, thorny tree, is another desert plant. These hardy plants can survive in desert areas that receive only 1 inch (2.5 cm) of rain per year.

Niger's southwestern corner, however, is home to a much wider variety of green life. Plants here include the fruit-bearing baobab tree. Its massive trunk is thick enough to hold large amounts of water. The far southwest is also home to towering kapok trees. In addition, Niger's oases often support a variety of plant life, including date palms. These tall trees sport clusters of sugary date fruit and can live for more than one hundred years.

Niger's animal life follows a similar pattern. Niger's desert areas can support only the toughest creatures. One of the rarest animals in the country—and in the world—is the addax. This light-colored antelope has long, twisting horns and a narrow face. The addax is highly adapted

An **addax** grazes on desert vegetation. Small green patches like this one spring up for short periods after rain.

to desert life. Its wide hooves and short legs help it walk across sand. It can handle the desert's high temperatures, partly by sleeping during the day and becoming active during the night. The addax can go most of its life without drinking, absorbing the moisture it needs from its diet of grasses, herbs, leaves of acacia trees, and other desert plants. Living in small groups, addaxes often travel long distances in search of these limited foods. Yet despite the animal's many adaptations, the addax is seriously endangered. Hunters kill addexes for their prized and beautiful horns. In addition, agriculture, mining, and other human activity have forced the dwindling addax population deeper into the harshest parts of the Sahara. Scientists believe only several hundred (or fewer) of the antelopes are alive.

Northern Niger is also home to the fennec, a small desert fox with reddish-gold fur and a bushy, black-tipped tail. Like the addax, the fennec has adapted to its harsh environment. Its very large ears help to move heat away from its body. In addition, the bottoms of the fennec's paws are covered with fur, protecting them from burning-hot desert sands. Fennecs are nocturnal, leaving their burrows at night to hunt insects, lizards, birds, and small rodents, as well as to eat roots and other plants. Also like the addax, the fennec faces threats. Hunters target the foxes for their fur, while trappers sell them as pets.

Southwestern Niger, in contrast, is home to typical West African animals such as elephants, lions, warthogs, impalas (a type of antelope), hyenas, hippopotamuses, water buffalo, and crocodiles. The area also supports a small population of the rare and disappearing West African giraffe. Many types of freshwater fish swim in the Niger River. West African manatees and spotted-necked otters also call the river home. The nation's skies host birds including grouse, doves, ravens, and larks. During the rainy season, migrating birds pass through the nation.

The Aïr Massif's relatively high precipitation levels and its hot springs make the mountains quite welcoming to wildlife. In addition, its harsh terrain helps keep people away, thereby protecting its plants and animals. Diversity of both plant and animal life here is high. Nigerien animals that inhabit the Aïr Massif include several types of gazelles, Barbary sheep, and snakes such as the sand viper and the African puff adder.

Natural Resources

Niger boasts several important natural resources. The largest and most valuable is uranium, a metal used in creating nuclear power. The massive uranium deposits concentrated in Niger's northwest are among the globe's largest, and Niger is in the world's top five producers of uranium.

Gold and salt—both of which have historically been important to the Nigerien economy—continue to be major resources. Others are petroleum and coal, as well as the metals tungsten, iron, and tin. Important mineral resources include gypsum (used in construction and in making fertilizer) and phosphate (used as a water softener).

Environmental Challenges

Niger faces a host of environmental challenges. First and foremost, the desert is growing. Throughout the Sahel region, the Sahara claims an average of about 16,000 square miles (41,440 sq. km) of land each year. This process is called desertification. Several factors contribute to desertification, including climate changes and drought. The impact of a growing human population—such as the overgrazing of livestock—also adds to desertification. Another major factor is deforestation—the clearing of trees and other vegetation. Loss of trees and root systems, in turn, causes soil erosion, which then contributes to further desertification. In addition, erosion along the Niger River's banks sends silt (tiny particles of rock and soil) into the water, threatening to clog this vital artery.

The Nigerien government has taken steps to slow the cycle, however. A tree-planting program has begun. In addition, efforts by individual farmers and other residents are focused attempts to conserve existing plant life. These efforts are making a difference. Reports in the early 2000s showed a rising number of trees and increased vegetation cover of more than 7 million square miles (18,129,917 sq. km) of land since about the 1970s. Work to protect the river by rebuilding banks and preserving riverside vegetation is also in progress.

November brings the harmattan to Niger. This dry, hot wind blows toward the southwest from the Sahara. It carries with it fine sand and dust, sometimes resulting in a thin haze that covers the land.

Threats to Niger's wildlife are another problem. To address this issue, the country's government has created national parks. The Réserve Naturelle Nationale de l'Aïr et du Ténéré (Aïr and Ténéré National Nature Reserve) covers a massive area in the Aïr Massif and Ténéré Desert. It protects a wide range of wildlife, including the addax. The highly endangered West African ostrich, whose population may be limited to just a few birds, may also live here. In all, scientists have recorded 40 mammal species, 165 bird types, and more than 15 types of reptiles in the reserve.

In Niger's far southwest lies a second national park and wildlife refuge, W National Park. Niger shares this protected area—shaped like the letter W—with Benin and Burkina Faso. About 850 square miles (2,201 sq. km) of it lie within Niger. This relatively lush area is home to lions, elephants, tortoises, and many other animals—including the endangered West African giraffe.

Uranium mining also has the potential to harm the environment. Uranium's radioactivity can contaminate water and land. Such contamination puts the health of plants, animals, and humans in danger. In the early 2000s, French inspectors reported that people living in and near Arlit (northern Niger's main uranium mine) were suffering from unexplained illnesses. They suggested that these diseases could be due to radiation from the site. Mining companies have pledged to tighten safety measures and to reduce peoples' exposure to radiation. But some observers believe that the danger is still high.

Visit www.vgsbooks.com for links to websites with additional information about Niger's geographical features. Explore the everyday life and famous sights of cities such as Niamey and Agadez, and learn about the lands traveled by caravans.

Cities

Niger's capital, Niamey, is by far the nation's largest city, with an estimated population of more than 700,000 people. It is located in the country's southwest and lies along the banks of the Niger River. The city became Niger's capital in 1926 and grew rapidly thereafter. Modern Niamey remains the nation's cultural, political, and economic hub. In addition to holding most of the Nigerien government, it is home to an airport, a university, and a national museum.

The nation's second-largest city is Zinder, with about 200,000 residents. Set in south central Niger, Zinder has been an important settlement since the 1700s, even serving as the nation's capital before Niamey. Lying southwest of Zinder is Maradi, Niger's third-largest city and home to more than 145,000 people. Maradi is a long-standing center of trade and commerce and is home to a daily market and a center for traditional crafts. Following a devastating flood in 1946, few buildings from Maradi's old town are still standing.

A merchant displays brightly colored beds for sale at a market in Zinder.

Agadez ranks as the next-largest city, home to at least 75,000 people. Set near the eastern foothills of the Aïr Massif, Agadez is considered the jumping off point and last major settlement before the expanse of the Ténéré Desert. This position as a gateway has made the city important for hundreds of years. Dating back to at least the fourteenth or fifteenth century, it once served as a crossroads of trading routes. In modern times, Agadez continues to be a major desert city, with traditional mud-brick homes and buildings, as well as a grand mosque (Islamic temple). The mosque's minaret (tower) stands more than 85 feet high (26 m), making it the tallest structure for a great distance in every direction.

In addition, small but important outposts, such as the east central town of Bilma, lie in eastern and northeastern Niger. Bilma, built around an oasis, was another stop for traders. Other remote northeastern towns include Djado, Madama, and Séguédine.

HISTORY AND GOVERNMENT

Niger has a rich and fascinating past. It has been an important part of northern and western Africa's history for many centuries.

Archaeologists and historians believe that people have been living in the northern part of present-day Niger for more than sixty thousand years. Historians estimate that by about 4000 B.C., settlers in Niger herded cattle. While the region was probably quite dry at the time, scientists believe that it was not as arid as it is in modern times.

Some of the early peoples left their mark on the region in creative ways. Dabous Rock in the Aïr Massif bears ancient images of two giraffes. The animals are carved into the sandstone rock. They are nearly life-sized at close to 20 feet (6 m) high, and the carvings are probably between six thousand and nine thousand years old. Other animal carvings and paintings also decorate the area's stone. But even the experts know few details about the earliest history of Niger, because written historical records from that time do not exist.

Caravan Culture

By the seventh century, heavily traveled trans-Saharan trading routes had evolved in the region that would one day become Niger. Trans-Saharan trade would remain a strong force in the area for centuries to come. Niger's strategic location between the Mediterranean Sea and the Gulf of Guinea (part of the Atlantic Ocean) made it a valuable hub of the bustling trade taking place across the Sahara. The trade routes crisscrossed the desert, connecting the Mediterranean and North Africa with the empires south of the Sahara. Several of them passed directly through Niger. Along these routes traveled caravans—chains of traders and camels. Many caravans were made up of at least one thousand camels and sometimes more than ten thousand. Camel herders often fattened up their animals before the journey, so that the animals could endure the grueling trek across the desert.

Guides led the caravans through the seas of shifting sands, where inexperienced travelers could easily lose their way. Caravans carried a

THE SALT OF THE EARTH

Slaves mined large amounts of salt from the Nigerien desert, carving great slabs of it. Salt was also obtained through evaporation (as water evaporates, it leaves its salt behind). Within the future nation of Niger, the best-known source of salt was Bilma. This oasis houses underground pools of salty water. When the water is exposed to the heat of eastern Niger's sun, it evaporates, leaving behind only the salt.

variety of goods. Some merchants, for instance, sold items such as leather and henna (a plant-based dye). Other goods traded included cloth, spices, and ivory. Slaves were also a commodity. Gold was one of the most valuable items. Mediterranean peoples desired large amounts of the precious metal, which workers extracted from mines primarily in western Africa.

Another product, salt, was less glamorous than gold but would become just as valuable to the trans-Saharan economy. Salt is a necessary mineral for the good health of both humans and animals. It is especially important in very hot regions, where the body sweats out much of its salt. Salt is also used to season food, as well as to preserve it. These qualities made the mineral extremely valuable. At some points in history, salt commanded prices as high as gold did.

Salt was a central part of the region's commerce. One of the major salt-producing cities was Bilma. In addition, Bilma lay on the caravan path between North Africa and the cities of southeastern Niger. Agadez, too, was a stopping point for merchants. It hosted caravans traveling from North Africa, across the Sahara, and into western Africa.

As caravans carried goods across the Sahara to the south, they also brought new beliefs. Beginning in the seventh century, the religion of Islam was one of the most important and influential ideas that traveling merchants introduced to northern and western Africa. Muhammad had founded the religion of Islam on the Arabian Peninsula (modern Saudi Arabia) in the A.D. 600s. From there, it spread quickly through most of the Middle East. Arab traders brought the faith—as well as the Arabic language—to North Africa. From there it spread southward into other areas of the continent.

◉ Ancient Realms

Several of the early kingdoms in Niger and the surrounding region were based on ethnic groups. For instance, in the 600s, a group known as the Hausa began setting up states in eastern Niger and the Aïr region. The Hausa people shared a language family. They also shared a

The **Djado Oasis** was once a station on the dangerous journey across the Sahara. Archaeologists do not know who lived at Djado, but they estimate that it was built between six hundred and one thousand years ago.

legend about seven Hausa states, each founded by one of seven sons born to a founding king and queen. These realms are sometimes called the Hausa Bakwai, or Hausa Seven. Leaders of a second group of seven states also claimed Hausa heritage. Most members of the Hausa Bakwai did not acknowledge these newer states as legitimate Hausa realms, however.

Other groups in the region also rose to power. The Songhai group, which is actually comprised of many smaller ethnic groups, called clans, arose in about the 700s. Their realm emerged in Gao, a city in what later became eastern Mali. By around 1000, another group called the Tuareg had migrated from the Sahara into the Sahal. The Tuareg comprised part of the large and varied Berber ethnic group of northern and northwestern Africa. They are traditionally a nomadic people, moving from place to place rather than living in permanent settlements. The Tuareg traveled across the desert, seeking water and vegetation for their camel herds. Tuareg groups moved gradually southward. By the 1100s, the they had moved into the Aïr Massif area and had forced many of the Hausa groups from the region. The Tuareg would go on to found a realm of their own, with Agadez as its hub.

By the thirteenth century, the Hausa states were a major regional power. But while some joined forces to create larger realms, the states remained largely independent of each other rather than forming a single unified empire. They often traded with each other and at first lived relatively peacefully together. Eventually, however, they came into conflict over power and territory.

Meanwhile, the Songhai realm had emerged as a full-fledged empire. Eventually, it grew to vast proportions. It controlled much of what later became southwestern Niger, as well as parts of Nigeria. At the Songhai's height, during the fifteenth and sixteenth centuries, it reached westward to the Atlantic Ocean.

Camels were critical to the caravan trade that crisscrossed Niger. These resilient animals can carry heavy loads and can go days without water. For these reasons, they are sometimes called ships of the desert.

The Kanem-Bornu Empire was also an important power. In the mid-thirteenth century, Kanem-Bornu gained a solid foothold in southeastern Niger and northeastern Nigeria, around Lake Chad. Kanem-Bornu peaked in power and territory in the late 1500s and early 1600s. As time went on, the various powers in Niger came into contact and sometimes conflict with one another, and some territory changed hands. For example, the Fulani people emerged as a power in the 1700s. This nomadic ethnic group was known for its expert horse riders, whom the group used to extend territory and power. Fulani forces threatened Kanem-Bornu in the 1700s. The following century, the Fulani also placed pressure on the Hausa states, eventually taking over Hausa land in southern Niger. Competition also arose with empires that lay beyond the future borders of Niger, such as the empires of Mali and Ghana to the west.

The influence of Islam only grew as the centuries passed. Many Fulani and Hausa leaders had embraced the faith. So had some of Kanem-Bornu's rulers. But the region's inhabitants already had their own sets of beliefs. These beliefs included animism, a religion that believes spirits reside within beings, natural objects such as mountains, and events such as weather. Most of the people were not quick to adopt the new religion. Most average Hausa, for instance, continued to follow their traditional faiths for several centuries more. In Kanem-Bornu, the spread of Islam caused friction between those who adopted the religion and those who did not. By the beginning of the nineteenth century, however, a majority of the area's realms and peoples had adopted Islam—at least to some degree. Many blended Islam with elements of animism.

European Exploration

Although caravan traffic remained heavy through Niger for hundreds of years, Europeans did not travel there until the nineteenth century. The first European to do so was Mungo Park, a Scottish explorer who arrived in 1805 or 1806. Park passed through Niger as part of a Niger River journey that took him farther into Africa's interior than any previous Europeans had reached.

Next came an expedition that included German explorer Heinrich Barth. Barth was a scholar of geology and archaeology, as well as an experienced adventurer. Traveling southward from Tripoli (in modern Libya) through the Sahara, he reached Agadez in the autumn of 1850.

Barth's journey left him out of touch with his associates back in Europe for so long that they feared the worst. Hoping to find him alive, they sent out a search party led by another German explorer, Eduard Vogel. Once Vogel had connected with Barth near Lake Chad, he traveled to Zinder.

These and other exploratory ventures into Africa opened the way to further travel. European rulers and merchants wanted to

This engraving of **nomadic people** moving camp appeared in the 1871 edition of Heinrich Barth's book.

THE LURE OF AGADEZ

In Heinrich Barth's book *Travels and Discoveries in North and Central Africa*, he described his fascination with the Nigerien city of Agadez. He wrote, "What can be more interesting than a considerable town . . . on the border of the desert and of the fertile tracts of an almost unknown continent, established there from ancient times, and protected as a place of rendezvous [meeting] and commerce between nations of the most different character, and having the most various wants?"

claim shares of the continent's rich natural and mineral resources. In the nineteenth century, significant European powers such as Great Britain, Portugal, Italy, France, and Germany competed fiercely to carve Africa into colonies. France laid claim to the region that would become Niger.

French Forces

French troops began claiming land in western Africa during the late 1800s and first entered Niger during the same period. One of the most significant early expeditions was the Mission Afrique Centrale (Central Africa Mission), which was organized to explore and possibly claim land between the Niger River and Lake Chad. Military officers Paul Voulet and Julien Chanoine led the group. The mission set out from Dakar (a city in the modern nation of Senegal) in late 1898. It reached Zinder in 1899. Along the way, the force clashed with local villagers—in some cases leading to many deaths on both sides.

Regional resentment of the French was high, both before and after Voulet and Chanoine's misson. Nevertheless, French soldiers continued to press into the region. France officially established the Territoire Militaire de Zinder (Military Territory of Zinder) in 1900. This area joined more extensive French holdings in western Africa. France expanded its claim in 1910, creating the Military Territory of Niger. The French made Zinder this territory's capital the following year.

Challenges continued to plague the region's inhabitants. Severe drought and famine struck in 1913, lasting for more than a year. In 1914 World War I (1914–1918) erupted among European nations, and some African colonies became involved in the conflict. But France maintained control over Niger, even as local opposition to French rule remained intense. Tuareg soldiers, in particular, fought fiercely against the outsiders. In 1916 the Tuareg staged a major uprising in the Aïr

The **Tuareg** maintained their nomadic lifestyle despite the creation of new national borders. In the early 1900s, this Tuareg man and his family considered both Niger and Algeria home.

Two **Hausa farmers** from Gangara pose with traditional farm tools in the 1920s. The French encouraged Nigeriens to adopt European ways, but people in remote areas did not always have access to modern equipment.

region, laying siege to a French fort in Agadez. Despite the Tuareg's resilience, however, their traditional swords were simply no match for the French military, which had more advanced equipment and arms. While hostility remained, violent confrontations lessened. A few years later, in 1922, the French government formally created the Colonie du Niger (Colony of Niger). Niamey became the colony's capital in 1926.

Colonial Culture

France ruled its African colonies from a central government located in Paris, France. The highest authorities remained in France, while a governor-general was stationed in Senegal (another colony in western Africa). Below this level were regional governors located in Niger and other colonial territories.

One of the French government's goals in Africa was to assimilate (absorb) its colonial subjects into French culture. Officials and workers established schools in Niger, teaching Nigerien children the French language and French ways. They also encouraged adults to speak French, adopt French styles of dress, and embrace French holidays and other customs. They rewarded local residents who adopted these and other French characteristics. The more assimilated a Nigerien became, the more opportunities and status he or she had. Those who were successful at the assimilation process earned the elite title of *évolué*, which means advanced in French. This status granted them privileges that other Nigeriens did not have. For instance, évolués (also sometimes called *assimilés*) were allowed to apply for French citizenship, which in turn gave them the right to vote. They also were excused from corvée. The corvée was forced labor that unassimilated residents—known as the *indigénat*—were required to perform. Tasks done in Niger as part of corvée included constructing railroads and government buildings.

◎ Drive for Independence

Niger's official status as a full-fledged colony did nothing to lessen local opposition to French rule. Independence movements, some connected to similar movements in other African colonies, arose almost immediately. These movements gathered greater momentum following World War II (1939–1945). France was among the countries involved in the war in Europe. In addition, the fighting spread across the Mediterranean Sea to parts of Africa. More than 100,000 soldiers from French-held Africa fought along with French troops. When the war ended in 1945, France was on the winning side. But the war's aftermath included renewed stirrings of unrest and calls for independence throughout the nation's African colonies.

Partly as a response to this discontent, a new French constitution in 1946 created the French Union. The union reclassified France's African territories as overseas departments rather than colonies. This new classification changed the status of colonial residents, who became citizens of France. They also gained greater (but still limited) participation in the French government. For example, beginning in 1946, Nigeriens could elect one of their citizens as a representative to the French National Assembly, a part of France's legislature.

That same year, a group of évolués in Niger formed the Parti Progrèssiste Nigérien (PPN). The PPN was part of a larger political party in French-held West Africa, and in its early years it took a strongly anti-French position. But as different ideas and goals developed among its members, the PPN splintered into a variety of smaller groups. One major offshoot arose in 1954, when PPN member Djibo Bakary founded a new party called the Union Démocratique Nigérienne (UDN). The UDN eventually took the name Sawaba.

Partly through the efforts of groups such as Sawaba, Niger gradually moved closer to independence from France. These efforts were especially effective because France was facing independence movements in its other African colonies during the same period. And while Niger did have some valuable natural resources, it offered fewer than many of France's other African colonies. As a result, French colonial officials began making a gradual shift toward more local self-government by Nigeriens. In 1956 Sawaba leader Djibo Bakary became the first mayor of the city of Niamey.

The political party Sawaba was named for a Hausa word meaning "independence" or "freedom."

Two years later, in 1958, the French Community replaced the French Union. In December of that year, Niger became an autonomous republic (a self-governing state) within the community.

And that same month, Hamani Diori became the state's prime minister. Diori was a former representative in the French National Assembly and a cofounder of the PPN. He was also the cousin—and political rival—of Djibo Bakary, who was popular among French officials.

Hamani Diori

Finally, on August 3, 1960, Niger officially became an independent nation. Hamani Diori became president, making him the first leader of a free Niger. But Diori's time in power would bring limits on democratic freedom. For example, he quickly put a single-party system into place, allowing only his own PPN to operate within the country.

Dissatisfaction with Diori soon arose. Members of the banned Sawaba political party—led by Diori's cousin Bakary, whom he had exiled (banished from Niger)—began taking violent measures against him. Guerrilla fighters (forces who practice unconventional warfare) carried out attacks against government border stations and other posts in 1964. The following year they attempted to assassinate Diori himself. But the president's troops quickly and harshly put down such opposition. In 1965 Diori was technically reelected. However, his political party remained the only one allowed by law, and he was the only candidate who ran for the office.

Famine and Friction

Challenges for Niger and its people mounted in the following years. Beginning in 1968, Niger and other nations in the Sahel region endured a devastating drought. Rainfall dwindled severely, dropping to less than half of normal levels in some parts of Niger. In the already small farmable areas of the nation's south, crops failed. And in northern Niger, where much of the population depended on cattle herding for their livelihood, many families watched their livestock die or grow so hungry that they could not produce milk. Thousands of people moved southward to find enough grazing land for their animals or to seek other ways of surviving. Many Tuareg had to abandon their nomadic lifestyle, instead settling around Agadez. Still other Nigeriens left their country for Nigeria or other neighboring nations, hoping to find better conditions there.

As the drought wore on—eventually lasting more than five years—food shortages set in. The government established centers to

People from a remote village crowd around a helicopter delivering food and water in 1973. During the **Sahel Drought** aid organizations struggled to get food to areas without good roads.

distribute food to those in need. But some officials kept the grain and other supplies for themselves, even as an estimated 200,000 people went without enough to eat. Some of the aid sent from foreign nations met the same fate. Many Nigeriens were furious with Diori and his government for doing too little to help them and to ease their suffering. In addition, corruption was rampant among government officials.

Nevertheless, Diori managed to hold onto his position for several more years. Finally, however, the opposition to him was too great. In 1974 a military coup led by army officer Seyni Kountché forced Diori from power. Kountché's forces placed Diori under arrest, along with many other government officials. Kountché himself took control of the nation as an unelected president, vowing to help Niger's people recover from the drought and food shortages where Diori's government had failed.

Kountché swiftly established a military government, suspending Niger's constitution and dissolving its legislature (called the National Assembly). In place of these systems, he set up the Supreme Military Council (CMS). This new governing body handled both executive and legislative duties and was made up of military officers. Kountché also made changes in Niger's relationship with France. While he kept things relatively friendly, he did request the removal of the French troops that remained in the nation.

Meanwhile, Kountché kept an iron grip on control and did not tolerate challenges to his rule. For example, he ordered that leaders of an attempted coup in 1976 be executed. And while one of his own coup's stated purposes had been to eliminate government corruption, Kountché himself took part in corrupt practices. He placed some of his own friends and family in powerful positions, and some members of his circle acquired vast wealth.

Kountché did take some steps to modify his regime, while never giving up his own power. For example, he gradually reduced the number of army officers in the government, replacing them with civilian (nonmilitary) members. In 1983 he also added the new position of prime minister, and the first person appointed to the office, Oumarou Mamane, was a civilian.

Kountché continued to face dissent and challengers, however. His troops squashed another attempted coup in 1983. The 1980s also brought a disastrous drop in uranium prices, seriously damaging Niger's economy. And in 1984, another drought struck the nation. Before successfully addressing any of these issues, Kountché died of a brain tumor in 1987.

Kountché's successor was his cousin Ali Saibou. Saibou had served as the army's chief of staff in Kountché's government. In 1989 voters took part in the first national elections held in Niger in nearly two decades. They chose Saibou as president—but they had no other choice, as no one else was allowed to run for the office. In the following months, Saibou faced internal friction. In February 1990, student demonstrations broke out in Niamey over reduced scholarship funding, calls for greater democracy, and other issues. Students refused to go to classes and organized a march through downtown Niamey. Government security forces responded to the protests with violence and in one incident fired guns into the crowd, killing at least ten students. Labor unions (organizations that fight for workers' rights) also protested. Union leaders called for better pay and conditions and organized a wave of strikes (work stoppages).

SCHOOL DAYS

The student uprisings that took place in 1990 were hardly the first stirrings of rebellion among Nigerien youth. Students in the nation had been organizing protests, strikes, and processions since the late 1960s. At times, schools were closed for weeks or months due to the unrest. In some cases students were arrested, occasionally along with teachers accused of participating in or supporting the protests.

Tuareg Discontent

Meanwhile, another challenge was growing urgent in northern Niger. Unrest had begun stirring among Tuareg groups. It was centered in the Aïr region, where most Tuareg lived. One reason for the turmoil was the return of thousands of Tuareg who had left the region during the drought, seeking greener pastures for their livestock. When they returned, the government promised to help them resettle in the Aïr region, but Tuareg communities argued that officials had not followed through on that promise. Another point of conflict was what the Tuareg saw as a long-standing disrespect for their land and culture by the central government in Niamey.

These tensions grew violent in May 1990, when a clash between Tuareg fighters and government forces erupted at Tchin-Tabaradene, a city not far from Tahoua. Tuareg soldiers had attacked a fort there, attempting to seize weapons. Security forces responded to the attack with violence and reportedly went on to target and kill Tuareg in the region—even those who had not had anything to do with the initial confrontation. How many died is the subject of much debate, with estimates ranging from about sixty to more than one thousand. In any case, the incident sparked a full-fledged Tuareg rebellion against the Nigerien government. Over the course of the late 1980s and the beginning of the 1990s, several different armed Tuareg groups emerged, defining themselves as liberation movements. They called for the removal of government troops from the Aïr region and a more autonomous Tuareg region within northern Niger.

This 1994 photograph shows Tuareg rebels of the Coordination of the Armed Resistance, a group fighting for the return of Tuareg land.

They wanted greater funds and other resources to be devoted to northern Niger. Some also hoped to gain protection of Tuareg culture, including the teaching of Tamashek, the Tuareg language, in schools.

In pursuit of these goals, armed Tuareg groups launched guerrilla attacks on government outposts. They also took hostages from government and police forces. In some cases, they attacked tourists in the Aïr and Ténéré regions.

Taking New Steps

Public outcries arose over the Tuareg rebellion, as well as over the 1990 student killings and other issues. In response, President Saibou agreed to hold a national conference on political reform in 1991. More than one thousand people, representing various parts of the Nigerien population, attended the conference. As a result of this three-month gathering, an interim (temporary) government replaced Saibou's. In 1992 Nigeriens voted in a new, more democratic constitution that allowed multiple political parties, protected freedom of speech, and limited presidential power. The following year, voters chose Mahamane Ousmane as president in Niger's first multiparty elections since independence. Ousmane became the nation's first Hausa president.

Suspicion of the government remained, however, and strikes and student demonstrations continued after Ousmane's election. In addition, reaching a settlement with Tuareg groups proved to be difficult, as no single leader or committee spoke for the various movements. In 1995, however, the Nigerien government signed a peace agreement and cease-fire with the Tuareg.

Ousmane also faced challenges from within his government, especially from Hama Amadou, who became prime minister in 1995. With the government locked in debates and tension, army officer Ibrahim Bare Mainassara took power through a military coup in January 1996. Mainassara and his soldiers placed Ousmane under arrest, along with Prime Minister Amadou. Pledging that he would restore political order that had broken down under Ousmane, Mainassara established a military junta (ruling council). The junta banned all political parties and suspended the constitution, but it promised an eventual return to civilian rule.

Visit www.vgsbooks.com for links to websites with additional information about Niger's government. Read about the president and prime minister and get the latest information on issues that concern Niger's people.

In the spring of 1996, the junta did introduce a new constitution, lifted the ban on political parties, and declared that open elections would take place. Mainassara also stated that he would run for president, and he faced four challengers for the position. But the July 1996 elections—which placed Mainassara in office—turned out to be largely for show. Mainassara had imprisoned his opponents. Many observers believed that the election had been rigged.

Mainassara's reign continued to be marked by corruption. In turn, his unpopularity continued to grow, and strikes and protests plagued him during the following years. Then, in April 1999, his power came to an abrupt and bloody end. As a military coup attempted to seize the government, Mainassara's own presidential guard killed him. Major Daouda Wanké took control. Another new constitution was approved later in 1999, restoring former democratic policies such as multiparty elections.

The next such election took place in autumn 1999, when Nigerien voters chose Mamdou Tandja as president. Outsiders saw the election as generally fair and peaceful, although fewer than half of Niger's eligible voters took part. Tandja's time in office began relatively smoothly but hit a rocky patch in the early 2000s, when protesters called for the nation to adopt Islamic law. Then, in 2002, soldiers in eastern Niger and in Niamey began to mutiny (rebel against their commanders), demanding better living conditions and pay. One of these uprisings lasted for ten days, ending only when other government troops stepped in.

In the early 2000s, more than 10 percent of Niger's National Assembly seats were held by women, who earlier had largely been excluded from political life.

Two years later, Niger reached a landmark. The nation's government had previously been limited to a federal body, without official regional or local governments. This situation changed in 2004, when Niger held its first local elections for members to serve in regional and local posts. Members of President Tandja's party won most of these new positions. That same year, Tandja was reelected president.

Ongoing Challenges

Niger's cycle of drought and famine soon hit the nation again. Serious food shortages had begun in the early 2000s. They resulted from a combination of low rainfall and massive swarms of locusts (grasshopper-like insects) that destroyed crops. The situation had reached crisis levels by 2005, as many thousands of Nigeriens faced malnutrition and starvation. Desperation among the people brought conflicts between nomads and farmers over land. As in the past, some residents left the country to seek better conditions. And like many previous leaders, President Tandja was criticized harshly for taking too little action to address the problem. By 2006 the United Nations (an international organization formed to help handle global issues) had reported that its World Food Program was helping feed 1.5 million people in Niger. Disastrous drought and famine continue to plague Niger and its residents.

Another past challenge reappeared in February 2007, when Tuareg fighters in northern Niger launched new attacks on military, government, and business targets. A group called the Niger Movement for Justice (MNJ) led these attacks. The MNJ claimed that the government had not followed through on promises made after the 1995 cease-fire. In particular, the MNJ called for Tuareg groups to receive a greater share of profit from natural resources in the north. As part of this goal, MNJ fighters focused many of their attacks on foreign businesses in Niger, especially those related to the nation's uranium industry. Meanwhile, the MNJ claimed that defectors from the army were swelling the group's ranks to nearly two thousand people. Despite some talks between MNJ members and government officials, this new wave of rebellion continued into the autumn of 2007.

◉ Government

Modern Niger's government is officially democratic. The 1999 constitution states that all citizens who are eighteen years of age and older have the right to vote. It also allows multiple parties and free elections.

Voters elect the president for a five-year term. The president, who is officially the head of state, can be reelected one time only. The president appoints the prime minister, who helps with the day-to-day running of the government.

Niger's legislative (lawmaking) body is the National Assembly, made up of 113 members. Like the president, these assembly members are elected by the people to serve five-year terms.

At the federal (national) level, the court system includes a Supreme Court of Justice, a Constitutional Court (to handle cases related to the constitution), and a Court of Appeals. A High Court of Justice tries the president and other government officials for any crimes they might have committed while in office. Smaller courts handle regional issues. Similarly, the country is divided into seven administrative departments, or districts, with regional and local leaders to govern Niger's people.

THE PEOPLE

Niger is home to 14.4 million people, giving the large nation a population density of 29 inhabitants per square mile (11 people per sq. km). In comparison, the neighboring country of Nigeria has a population density of 377 people per square mile (145 per sq. km). In the United States, an average of 80 people live in each square mile (31 per sq. km). Because about one-fifth of Niger's residents live in urban areas, however, Niamey and other cities are more crowded than this number suggests. The country's vast desert areas, on the other hand, have very low concentrations of people.

Ethnic Groups

Niger is home to people claiming a wide variety of ethnic backgrounds. These ethnicities are not limited by the modern nation's borders but instead spread across boundaries throughout the regions of the Sahel and northwestern Africa.

Most Nigeriens are of Hausa heritage, with about 55 percent of the

population falling into this category. Subgroups also exist within the large Hausa ethnicity. Some of these include the Adarwa, Konnawa, and Gobirawa. Many of these divisions are based on the ancient Hausa states that once ruled in precolonial Niger. The Hausa have historically been excellent traders and merchants, as well as working in farming or skilled crafts such as textile making. In modern times, Hausa people hold a wide variety of jobs and careers.

The second largest ethnic group in Niger is actually made up of two separate groups, the Songhai and the Djerma. They are usually grouped together due to long-standing historical and geographical links. Together they make up about 21 percent of Niger's population. Most live near the Niger River, and many make their living in farming and fishing. Like the Hausa, the Songhai-Djerma group has many subdivisions, such as the Gaba, Kado, Tinga, and Sorko. Also like the Hausa, some of these smaller groups have links to realms in early Niger.

About 9 percent of Nigeriens have Tuareg ancestry, with most living in the Aïr Massif region. The Tuareg have a reputation as fiercely independent and proud of their nomadic past. While some have adapted to a partially settled lifestyle in modern Niger, nomadic traditions are still very important to Tuareg culture. Tuareg society is based on family associations, clans, and larger groups. In addition, Tuareg society traditionally follows a strict class system, dividing the people into nobles, commoners, and slaves. A person's class once determined what he or she could do for a living. Historically, for example, people among the highest social group could work in the caravan trade—a very profitable business. Some of the lower groups, by contrast, had to work in more labor-intensive jobs, such as making and repairing tools and other goods.

Another 9 percent of the population is Fulani. Like the Tuareg, most Fulani are traditionally cattle herders. Although they were once nomadic, few follow this lifestyle in modern times. Instead, most Fulani families have settled down in towns and cities. Within the Fulani group are the Wodaabe, also sometimes called the Bororo. Unlike most Fulani, the Wodaabe continue a traditional nomadic existence, moving primarily through the area around Tahoua and Agadez. They raise livestock including zebu cattle, goats, donkeys, and camels and continue to travel to find water and food for their herds. The most

THE DESERT BLUES

Tuareg males are sometimes nicknamed the "blue men" of the desert. The name arose because they traditionally wrapped their heads and faces in cloth to protect themselves from the desert heat. The cloth was usually stained with blue indigo dye, which often rubbed off on the wearer's face.

A Tuareg man directs a caravan from camelback. He wears the traditional **indigo-dyed veil** and dark robes.

A Wodaabe woman milks a zebu cow while a man holds the animal's horn. **Zebu cattle** are thought to be the oldest breed of domesticated cattle.

important animals in their culture are the zebu cattle, whose milk is an important staple of the Wodaabe diet. Wodaabe families live in small shelters that they build from branches. These homes are open to the desert sky and are easily moved or rebuilt with each migration.

Smaller Nigerien ethnic groups include the Kanuri, located mostly in eastern Niger and making up about 4 percent of the nation's people. The Toubou make up about another 1 percent. There are also small populations of Arabs, as well as European immigrants (most of them from France), who together amount to about 1 percent of the total population. Over the years, some intermarrying among different ethnicities has taken place, especially between Tuareg and French people.

Language

Niger's official language is French—a clear remnant of the nation's colonial period. But most of the country's ethnic groups and subgroups have their own languages. Dozens of different tongues are spoken throughout the region. Most Nigeriens speak French as well as at least one more language.

As the language of the largest ethnic group, Hausa is the most common local language. It has also been adopted by non-Hausa residents of Niger. The Hausa tradition of working in trade spread the language through Niger and beyond. At the same time, the Hausa tongue absorbed many Arabic words over the centuries. Djerma is another

LANGUAGE LESSON

Learn how to say "thank you" in some of Niger's major languages.

French:	*merci*
Hausa:	*yawwa*
Djerma:	*ngoyya*
Tamashek:	*tanimert*

A Tuareg boy practices reading French at a **traveling classroom.** Such schools teach the children of nomadic peoples as they travel.

major language in Niger, while Tuareg people speak Tamashek and Fulani people speak Fulfulde.

Education

In modern Niger, public education is free and is required by law for children between the ages of seven and fifteen. In practice, however, few children actually attend school. In the early 2000s, some reports stated that only about 40 percent of school-aged children went to classes. In addition, funding of schools has been a problem. Often teachers and schools lack enough books and other resources. The literacy rate—the number of Nigeriens fifteen years of age and older who can read—hovers between 15 and 20 percent. Literacy is higher among Nigerien men than women. Many Nigeriens traditionally have only educated their sons, while daughters stayed home to learn housekeeping and other domestic skills. Cultural and religious beliefs continue to limit many girls' access to education. Overall, Niger's literacy rate is among the lowest in the world.

Education has long been relatively limited in Niger. One reason is that because much of the nation is so sparsely populated, huge distances exist between people and schools. Diversity among ethnic groups presents additional challenges. For instance, nomadic groups that move from place to place have difficulty keeping their children in one school.

A variety of international organizations are working to improve education in Niger. These groups build schools, provide classrooms and teachers with the materials they need, and encourage families to send their girls to school. Niger's own government has also set up programs to improve the nation's educational system. One such program focuses specifically on increasing the number of female students. Others are aimed at raising literacy rates.

For students who complete primary and secondary school, several options exist for higher education. The nation's main institution of higher education is the Abdou Moumouni University in Niamey (also called the University of Niamey). In addition, the city of Say is home to the Islamic University of Niger. Colleges and vocational schools train teachers and provide students with skills in areas such as craft-making.

City Life, Country Life

All over the country, from Niamey to the smallest village, many people live in very modest homes. Most of these are built of sun-dried mud bricks. They are generally simple, square shapes. Most are a single story high. Niamey is home to some larger and more modern buildings, such as apartment complexes and homes built from concrete and other materials. But the reliable mud structure is still common. Rural families in crop-

DRESSED FOR THE DESERT

Some Nigeriens in Niamey and some other cities have adopted European-style clothing, such as suits and jeans. But many people throughout Niger still wear traditional clothing. Most of these styles are adapted to the desert's harsh climate. These styles feature long, flowing garments, which protect against the sun, hot desert winds, and blowing sand. Cloth wrapped around the head and sometimes over the face provides similar protection. And when night falls and temperatures plummet, these clothes also provide warmth. Some variations do exist from group to group, however. Tuareg people are famous for their vivid blue robes. The Hausa—especially men—often favor robes and caps with intricate embroidered patterns. Hausa women traditionally wear colorful wraparound skirts and blouses, along with a cloth tied around their hair. Fulani people also wear brightly colored and sometimes patterned clothing, and men in particular like to wear jewelry. Men also wear caps, while most women wear veils when they leave their houses, according to Islamic guidelines.

growing regions also have separate buildings to hold grain. These structures are also usually built of mud and are typically round.

A TROUBLING TRADITION

A major human rights concern in Niger is the issue of slavery. The practice has a long history in Niger and throughout the region. A new chapter of that history opened when the slave trade began between the Americas and Africa in the 1500s. When the French colonized Niger, they outlawed slavery. Not all ethnic groups adhered to the ban, but many slaves did gain their freedom or escape from their masters. Slavery continued in parts of Niger, however, lasting after the nation achieved independence and even into the twenty-first century. It is especially common in Tuareg communities that continue to follow the centuries-old class system. The lowest group, or caste, is the *bellah*. Bellah members are born into their position. They are forced to work from childhood without pay for higher-caste Tuareg— often at risk of being beaten if they disobey. Niger's 1999 constitution formally prohibits slavery. Nevertheless, some international groups estimate that thousands of people still work as unwilling and unpaid laborers in Niger.

Among groups who still lead nomadic lifestyles, homes are light and easy to put up and take down. Nomadic Tuareg and Fulani, for example, build dwellings that are supported by wooden poles and covered with cloth, goatskins, or mats woven from plant matter.

In Niamey, Zinder, and other large cities, many adults go to daily jobs in government, in tourism-related businesses, or in other areas. A larger proportion of city children go to school than in rural areas, and in Niamey, university students bustle to and fro. Cars and motor scooters are relatively common in the nation's bigger cities, and jeeps and SUVs cross the desert stretches between towns. But vehicles are fewer in the countryside, where people often still travel on foot or by camel. Camels and donkeys also haul goods from place to place. Large animals walking through the streets are still a common sight even in Niamey.

In small villages and in rural areas—where homes do not have running water or electricity— many families devote their days mostly to completing the tasks necessary for getting by. These jobs include gathering water from wells or oases, leading livestock to graze, and preparing food. Every family member has duties. In fact, many children—especially outside of Niamey—do not go to school because they are helping their families with this work.

Most Nigerien women fill traditional roles within their families, but a growing number hold jobs in business and civil service. In 2005 Niamey introduced an **all-female police squad.** This officer is directing traffic.

Women's Roles and Struggles

In Nigerien culture, women have traditionally held clearly defined roles within the family and the community. Especially in many rural ethnic groups, women are usually responsible for caring for the family home, rearing children, and preparing meals. In nomadic groups such as the Wodaabe, women also tend the camp, build the family shelter, and milk the livestock.

Despite this important role in family life, Nigerien women face many challenges. Niger's constitution officially forbids discrimination against all people. But in practice many women deal with prejudice and discrimination in finding work or getting equal pay to men. Women often face limited freedom to make choices about marriage and childbearing as well. In some ethnic groups—especially those in rural areas—families arrange marriages for their daughters at about the age of thirteen.

Extreme interpretations of Islam also play a role in restricting women's rights. Islam traditionally restricts women's freedom. For example, some Muslims (people who practice the Islamic faith) in Niger believe that women should not be allowed to divorce their husbands. Those women who do succeed in getting divorces face extra challenges in finding jobs or owning property. Some divorced women are even forced into prostitution to support themselves.

Women's participation in politics and government—both locally and nationally—has also been limited for many years. However, more

The women of **Dan Bako village,** near the town of Aguie, attend a community meeting. Aid organizations often offer classes about nutrition at such meetings, because women prepare and sometimes grow all of a family's food.

and more women have begun to vote in modern Niger. Women also hold National Assembly and other government offices.

Health

Niger's health statistics are among the worst in the world. Average life expectancy in the nation is 44 years. In contrast, residents of France are born with an average life expectancy of 80 years—nearly twice that of Nigeriens. The infant death rate is equally sobering, with 149 babies out of every 1,000 dying before the age of one. This figure is considerably higher than West Africa's average of 109 deaths for every 1,000 live births.

A major reason for these grim figures is the persistent problem of malnutrition. Access to freshwater is also a problem for many Nigeriens, even when the nation is not suffering from drought. And only 43 percent of people living in urban areas have access to good sanitation (waste removal). Outside of the cities, that number drops to 4 percent. These issues contribute to the spread of waterborne diseases such as typhoid fever and meningitis.

In addition to these challenges, hospitals and clinics are few and far between in Niger. Those that exist are dramatically understaffed, with an estimated ratio of 1 doctor for every 50,000 citizens. Medical facilities also lack good equipment, medicine, and other necessities.

Visit www.vgsbooks.com for links to websites with news about Niger's continuing efforts to fight famine and child mortality. Learn about the aid organizations that work with Nigeriens to get help to remote areas.

Despite Niger's many health care problems, the nation does boast low rates of HIV/AIDS (human immunodeficiency virus/acquired immunodeficiency syndrome). Throughout the population, only about 1 percent of Nigeriens have the virus.

Niger's government and international organizations are taking steps to improve the health of Niger's people. In 2003 President Tandja promised to build one thousand health centers, and by 2006 that goal was within reach. However, many of the new clinics did not have sufficient supplies.

Many Nigeriens turn to traditional methods of healing when they are sick or hurt. Some ethnic groups have treated patients with plant-based remedies for centuries, making medicines out of leaves, bark, and other natural ingredients.

A nurse at a **nutrition center** takes a blood sample from a malnourished child. These mothers and children are from Dogo, a village near Zinder. The area faces famine after severe drought killed most of the region's crops.

CULTURAL LIFE

As home to members of many different ethnic groups, Niger boasts a diverse cultural life. These groups bring together a variety of traditions, from ancient religious beliefs to modern music. Together, they continue to enrich modern Nigerien culture.

▶ Religion

The dominant religion in Niger is Islam, with about 85 to 90 percent of all Nigeriens identifying themselves as Muslims. The prophet Muhammad founded this religion on the Arabian Peninsula in the A.D. 600s. Muslims obey the Five Pillars of Islam, which instruct them to declare their faith, to pray, to fast (not eat or drink on certain days), to give to the poor, and to make a journey to Mecca (Islam's holy city). The two major subgroups within Islam are Sunni and Shiite. Most Nigeriens are part of the larger Sunni group.

About 8 to 13 percent of Nigeriens follow ancient belief systems, many of which are animist. Animism is based on the idea that spirits—

often called genies—inhabit the natural world. These spirits may be good or evil, and they can influence human lives and events.

The commonly reported percentages of Muslims and animists are somewhat misleading, however, as many Nigeriens participate in both faiths. As Islam entered Niger hundreds of years ago, many local peoples blended elements of the new religion with their traditional beliefs. This overlap continues in modern Niger.

About 2 percent of the population is Christian, and most of these people are Catholic. Christianity came to Niger with European missionaries (religious workers) in the early twentieth century.

Holidays and Festivals

Muslims celebrate Islamic holidays such as the holy month of Ramadan. Because Islamic holidays follow the lunar calendar, the date of Ramadan changes each year. This period is one of the most sacred times of the year for Muslims, who observe it by fasting

SPEAKING WITH SPIRITS

The best known group of animists in Niger are called the Azna, most of whom are Hausa people. Azna animists believe that genies have knowledge of the future. Azna soothsayers, or fortune tellers, carry out ceremonies in which they read signs and symbols—such as patterns in the sand—to predict the future. The Bori subgroup of the Azna also believe that spirits and gods can possess (take over) the bodies of humans—almost always women—and speak through them.

between sunrise and sunset. The month is a time for prayer, services at mosques, and quiet contemplation. However, it is also a festive time. After sundown, a meal called the *iftar* breaks the day's fast. Friends and families meet in the evening to share this meal together. Muslims all over the world mark the end of Ramadan with a magnificent feast and festival called Eid-al-Fitr. In Agadez, for example, leaders on horseback ride ahead of processions of people winding through the streets in celebration.

Eid-al-Adha—also known in Niger as Tabaski—is another important Islamic holiday. The festival commemorates a story in the Quran (Islam's holy book). It also celebrates the annual hajj, a pilgrimage to the Islamic holy city of Mecca, Saudi Arabia. According to Islam, all Muslims must try to make this journey once in their lifetime.

Nigerien Christians mark major holidays, including Christmas and Easter. In addition, many Nigerien holidays are based on cultural and ethnic traditions. One such event is the Cure Salée, which takes place near the end of the rainy season. It was historically an annual trip leading Tuareg cattle to large salt deposits located near Ingal, a city about 70 miles (113 km) west of Agadez. There, the animals could get the salt and minerals they needed—literally, they could take the *cure salée*, or "salt cure." Some herders traveled more than 200 miles (322 km) to reach the salt flats. In modern Niger, this traditional trek has expanded to include a large festival that brings together nomadic peoples from around Niger and beyond. Participants sell goods, trade or sell camels and other animals, watch camel races, enjoy music and dancing, and socialize. The celebration can last as long as a week and often draws close to ten thousand people—including nomads as well as other participants.

Also taking place after the rains is Geerewol, a Wodaabe festival. Several Geerewol gatherings may take place during this time period, scattered throughout the region around Agadez and Ingal. The most famous Geerewol ceremony is a dance celebrating the beauty of the young, unmarried Wodaabe men. These youths dress in elaborate clothing and jewelry for the event. They also apply striking makeup, coloring their skin with red and yellow powders, darkening their lips, lining their eyes in black, and drawing patterns of red and white lines and dots on their faces.

Once they are ready, the men dance to music provided by a chorus of singers. The slow dance involves feet stamping, chanting, and dramatic facial expressions. As the crowd watches, young unmarried women in the audience have the opportunity to single out the men who most appeal to them. These pairings sometimes lead to marriage, though they do not have to.

Niger also has a number of secular (nonreligious) holidays that mark political and historical events. August 3, for instance, is Independence Day, celebrating Niger's 1960 independence from France. Concord Day, on April 24, marks the 1995 agreement between the government and Tuareg groups. Other national holidays include New Year's Day on January 1 and Labor Day on May 1.

Musical Life

Music has long been important in Niger's culture, and it continues to thrive in the modern nation. Traditional and ethnic forms include the singing that accompanies the Wodaabe Geerewol ceremony and

Dressed in fine clothing and jewelry, young Wodaabe men dance at a **Geerewol** festival. Some grin and roll their eyes to emphasize their features.

A Nigerien woman plays the **goge,** a one-stringed instrument played by many cultures across West Africa.

Tuareg love songs. The most basic of all instruments for much ethnic music—especially that of nomadic groups—are hands for clapping, feet for stomping, and voices for singing. A variety of drums, such as the *tinde* drums that usually accompany Tuareg women's songs, are also used. Other traditional musical instruments include the Hausa *molo* (a three-stringed lute), *goge* (a fiddlelike stringed instrument), and *kakaki* (a brass trumpet). An important Fulani instrument is the flutelike *seyse*.

Dan Gourmou was a singer and composer from Tahoua. Before his death in 1980, he was famous for singing songs that sound similar to American blues music. He also encouraged the development of new musical styles in Niger. A musical contest and a festival named for him still take place in Tahoua every two years. The festival usually features *musique tradi-moderne*, a form that blends traditional music with modern styles and instruments. The musical group Etran Finawata uses this combination. They mix traditional nomadic music, such as Wodaabe chanting, with modern instruments such as electric guitar. Another popular band—and probably the best known outside of Niger—is Mamar Kassey. They combine musical sounds from Niger's many ethnic groups, using influences from the Hausa, Songhai, Fulani, and more. They also use traditional instruments and arrange their songs to modern beats to create lively tunes.

Rap is also popular among young Nigeriens. The nation's regional rap and hip-hop style is called Rap Nigerien. It grew rapidly in the late 1990s and early 2000s. Like so much music in Niger, it draws on traditional melodies and sometimes uses traditional instruments. Its lyrics, however, are often outspoken or even angry. Often spoken in a blend of Nigerien languages, they tackle subjects that concern Nigerien youth, such as poverty and government corruption. Two well known Rap Nigerien groups are WassWong and Kamikaz. Another artist, Zara Moussa, was West Africa's first female rap artist to record an album. Her lyrics speak out about discrimination against women as well as other social issues and problems in Niger.

Literature and Film

Western Africa and northern Africa—including Niger—are home to a long-standing storytelling tradition. Most stories explain natural wonders or events, or they teach lessons and values important to the culture. In Niger and other nearby nations, musical storytellers called griots (men) or *griottes* (women) often sing these tales. In the past, before reading and writing were common skills amongst Nigeriens, griot songs were especially important for keeping a historical record. The griot profession is usually passed down from generation to generation.

In postcolonial Niger, the most famous and productive author near the time of independence was Boubou Hama. Hama was a teacher and a scholar. He was also a political figure, as a founder and former leader of the PPN. He wrote more than fifty books in French, covering topics from history to philosophy, as well as works of fiction. Another author writing at about the same time was Mamani Abdoulaye, a journalist who also published poetry, a novel, and several plays.

Some Nigerien authors highlight their nation's vibrant ethnic mixture. For example, the Tuareg writer Hawad is a contemporary poet. He writes in the Tuareg language of Tamashek but also translates his work into French. His poems address issues facing nomadic cultures in modern Niger.

Literature faces a unique challenge in a nation where only a small percentage of people can read. As a result, nonwritten forms of storytelling, including film and theater, are important. Some filmmakers and authors have also cooperated to bring written works to the screen. Pieces by both Hama and Abdoulaye, for instance, have been adapted into films.

The earliest filmmaker in Niger was French. Jean Rouch arrived in Niger in the 1940s to do engineering work, but he made his mark as a documentary filmmaker (often filming the customs and rituals of West

A MUSICAL EDUCATION

Rap Nigerien is more than just entertaining. Musicians also use their art to educate Niger's people and bring about social change. In 2005 a group of more than forty rap and hip-hop artists spent a month traveling through the country. Their shows attracted thousands of people—in some cases drawing audiences of ten thousand at a time. As part of their performances, these musicians spoke and sang about important issues such as AIDS, women's rights, and the plight of hungry and homeless children in Niger.

African peoples). Rouch went on to help local artists get their start in film. For example, Oumarou Ganda first worked with Rouch as an assistant and went on to become a director as well as an actor. His work often portrays Nigerien life with a critical but also understanding perspective. His first movie, the 1969 film *Cabascabo*, won a number of international prizes, including one at France's prestigious Cannes Film Festival. Moustapha Alassane is another filmmaker who learned about moviemaking from Rouch. Alassane has made animated films, documentaries, and other movies. Limited resources and education continue to make it difficult to make movies in contemporary Niger, however. In 2006 the United Nations sponsored a film forum in Niamey. The event included a workshop for young people and was designed to help a new generation of Nigerien filmmakers get started in the art.

Live theater is another form of storytelling in Niger. One of its unique and popular attractions is the Pilotobé Festival. Made up of a traveling group of actors and other artists, the festival brings stage productions, storytelling, and other artistic performances to Agadez, Zinder, and other cities and towns.

Crafts and Visual Arts

Craftspeople create many artistic works in Niger. Tuareg men, for example, make beautiful silver jewelry. Such jewelry is a sign of wealth and status, and Tuareg women often wear these creations to celebrations such as weddings.

A group of **griots** from Agadez celebrate Eid-al-Fitr, the end of Ramadan, with songs and storytelling.

This collection of **Tuareg crosses** includes the Cross of Agadez *(top row, first from left).*

Nigerien craftspeople also make high-quality leather goods. Tuareg women decorate leather bags, sandals, and other items with intricate designs. Nigerien women create woven mats and baskets from palm leaves and similar natural materials, dyed to create colorful patterns. The Hausa are famous for making dyed cloth, especially long, brightly colored robes called boubous. Some groups hand-embroider their fabrics, while the Tuareg produce trademark cloth dyed with vivid blue indigo.

SILVER SYMBOLS

Cross shapes are common designs in Tuareg jewelry, especially in necklaces. Tuareg silversmiths create more than twenty different cross designs, each associated with a certain town or place. The most famous is the Cross of Agadez. Historically, these crosses—which have little if any relation to the Christian symbol—were passed down within families and showed where a Tuareg person came from.

European-style art is less common than traditional art in Niger, but some Nigeriens do create paintings and other works. For instance, Rissa Ixa is a Tuareg painter whose pieces show livestock herding, Tuareg camps, and other scenes from nomadic culture. To help expand artistic activity in the nation, Ixa established the Association for the Promotion and Development of Traditional Nomadic Arts and Cultures in Niger. Other Nigerien painters include Boubacar Boureima, who creates bright, abstract works.

Architecture

Niger's architecture reflects the same diversity that marks the rest of its cultural and social life. Throughout the nation, one of the most common building styles is simple and traditional. Sturdy buildings

A Hausa woman waits in the doorway of an elaborately **painted house** in Zinder.

with mud walls and flat roofs stand in Niamey and other large cities, as well as in smaller and more rural settlements. In some places, the brown walls are painted bright colors. And during the hottest and driest months of the year, many people seek cooler air by sleeping on their roofs, under the stars.

Other Nigerien styles include Hausa architecture. Also constructed of claylike mud, Hausa buildings are famous for their beautifully decorated outside walls. Zinder's Birni neighborhood has many impressive examples of this style. Although many have begun to deteriorate over time, work to restore them is under way.

Islam has influenced architecture in Niger, with mosques dotting the country. These places of worship vary considerably in style, however. Niamey's Grande Mosquée (Big Mosque) is a large building with bright white walls, gleaming bluish-green domes, and a tall, slender minaret (tower). By contrast, the older Agadez mosque, also called the Grande Mosquée, is a tan-colored mud structure, and its famous minaret is a wide, tapering rectangular shape. Wooden poles, which are commonly used for structural support in this architecture style (often called Sudanic), stick out on every side of the minaret.

French control brought some newer European building styles. Niamey in particular boasts a number of larger buildings, most of which house government offices. And in the 1970s, as money flowed into the nation from the uranium boom, new construction began. For example, a huge hotel in Niamey reflects this brief period of prosperity. But when uranium prices plunged, some of these structures fell into disrepair.

▶ Sports

Sporting events in Niger include a traditional style of wrestling that is widely seen as the national sport. An annual championship often draws tens of thousands of spectators. Competitions generally open with music and sometimes prayers. Once the match begins, two male opponents face each other, often wearing good luck charms. The main

Nigerien wrestler Kane Dembele *(right)* throws a French wrestler known as Le Meur *(center)* in a **Nigerien wrestling** match in Niamey.

goal is simply to knock down the opponent, which can happen in just a few seconds. Before making contact, wrestlers often circle each other and attempt to intimidate or surprise their opponent.

French influence in Africa brought soccer to the region, and more than a dozen Nigerien cities have teams. They include Niamey's Sahel SC, Zinder's Espoir FC, and Agadez's Urana FC d'Arlit. These teams play each other in local matches and nationwide competitions such as the Niger Cup. A number of stadiums around the country host these games. A stadium in Niamey holds more than thirty thousand people. Niger also has a national team, called the Mena. Led by coach Hamey Amadou, it plays against teams from other African nations. It has rarely qualified for major competitions such as the World Cup.

Other pastimes reflect traditional lifestyles. For example, the Tuareg people enjoy camel races, which often occur on holidays.

Food

Nigerien menus vary according to ethnic groups and geography. For instance, dishes and foods introduced by the French, such as steaks and French bread, are especially common in restaurants in Niamey and other cities. Nigeriens in the nation's southwest, near the Niger River, make fish a common part of their diet. Fresh fruit and vegetables are also more common in the relatively fertile south. Other regional and ethnic specialties include a cheese made by Tuareg and Fulani. Called *tchoukou* in the Hausa language and *takomért* in Tamashek, the cheese

A Wodaabe child watches as his father pours tea. Sharing tea with visitors is a sign of hospitality, and Wodaabe men carry tea sets with them as they travel.

may be made from the milk of goats, sheep, cows, or camels. A popular food around the southern city of Maradi is *kilichi*, thin, sun-dried slices of beef that are salted or spiced with hot pepper.

Some foods are common throughout the nation. Millet is a major ingredient in the diet of most rural residents. Cooks pound the grain into fine pieces and then boil it to create a thick porridge. They then season the dish with sauce made from their available ingredients. Often a bit spicy, this sauce may include vegetables such as okra, or—in prosperous times—meat. Mutton (sheep meat) is a favorite, especially for holidays and other special occasions.

Other starchy staples include corn, beans, couscous, noodles, and rice. Because of the ever-looming threat of drought and food shortages, filling dishes are highly valued by most Nigeriens. Desert groups also make a wheat bread that they bake in the embers of an open fire.

Some common Nigerien sweets are sweetened peanuts, common around Maradi, or a fudgelike candy made from sesame seeds called *halawa*. Beverages include milk—sometimes served curdled or in yogurt form—and juices made from plants such as hibiscus flowers and ginger. The most common Nigerien drink, however, is tea. Traditionally, tea is served according to a old ritual. Tea makers combine tea leaves, hot water, and sugar in an enamel pot, and pour the tea into small glasses. The same tea and sugar is then brewed again with a second round of water, and finally a third time. Each round is sweeter than the previous one. A popular saying goes that the first glass is as bitter as death, the second is as mild as life, and the third is as sweet as love.

OKRA AND CORNMEAL PORRIDGE

Made with cornmeal, this porridge and sauce dish is similar to meals that many Nigeriens eat almost every day.

2 tablespoons oil

1 large onion, chopped

2 cloves garlic, chopped finely

2 medium tomatoes, chopped

6 tablespoons tomato paste

1 teaspoon black pepper

½ teaspoon salt

½ teaspoon cumin

½ teaspoon cayenne powder

1 package (10 ounces) frozen okra, thawed

1 cup cornmeal

3 cups water

1. Put the oil and onion in a medium-sized pot. Fry over medium-high heat for about 5 minutes, or until soft. Add garlic and fry another 1 to 2 minutes.
2. Add tomatoes, tomato paste, black pepper, salt, cumin, and cayenne to the onions and garlic. Mix well, and simmer on low heat for 5 minutes.
3. Put okra in a blender, and blend until it becomes a thick paste. Add okra to ingredients in pot and simmer over low heat for 15 to 20 minutes, while you prepare the porridge. Stir occasionally.
4. In a bowl, mix cornmeal with 1 cup of the water.
5. Add remaining 2 cups of water to a medium-sized pot. Bring to a boil over high heat. Add cornmeal mixture to boiling water, and cook over medium heat for 10 to 15 minutes, stirring constantly, until mixture becomes a thick porridge.
6. Place okra mixture over cornmeal porridge and serve hot.

Serves 6

Visit www.vgsbooks.com for links to websites with more recipes from Niger and West Africa. Follow links to other websites and listen to samples of Nigerien music, including works by Mamar Kassey, and see examples of Nigerien arts and crafts.

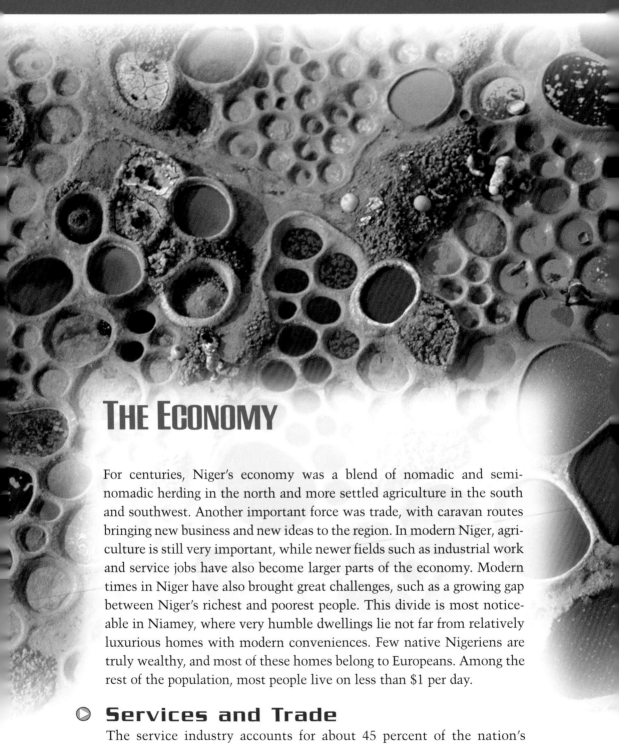

THE ECONOMY

For centuries, Niger's economy was a blend of nomadic and semi-nomadic herding in the north and more settled agriculture in the south and southwest. Another important force was trade, with caravan routes bringing new business and new ideas to the region. In modern Niger, agriculture is still very important, while newer fields such as industrial work and service jobs have also become larger parts of the economy. Modern times in Niger have also brought great challenges, such as a growing gap between Niger's richest and poorest people. This divide is most noticeable in Niamey, where very humble dwellings lie not far from relatively luxurious homes with modern conveniences. Few native Nigeriens are truly wealthy, and most of these homes belong to Europeans. Among the rest of the population, most people live on less than $1 per day.

Services and Trade

The service industry accounts for about 45 percent of the nation's gross domestic product. (The gross domestic product, abbreviated as

GDP, is a measure of the total annual value of goods and services produced by a nation's workers.) Services that fall into this sector include government work, banking, insurance, health care, and retail sales. About 4 percent of Niger's workers do jobs in this area.

The service sector is one of the most rapidly growing areas of the Nigerien economy. Tourism is one important reason for this growth. The Ténéré Desert's wild beauty and the romance of Tuareg towns such as Agadez attract many visitors each year. Popular tours retrace caravan routes and visit oases.

Niger imports goods from around the world. It buys most of these imports from France, the United States, the African nations of Côte d'Ivoire (Ivory Coast) and Nigeria, and Asian countries such as China and Japan. Main imports include food, vehicles and other machinery, and petroleum products. Niger exports products such as uranium and live animals, sending most of them to Nigeria, France, and Japan.

⊙ Agriculture

Agricultural jobs make up the second-largest portion of Niger's GDP, at about 42 percent. This measurement takes into account a wide variety of jobs that use the land, including farming and livestock herding, as well as forestry and fishing. This broad agricultural category employs the vast majority of Niger's working population, with about 90 percent of them doing jobs in this sector.

Nigerien farmers raise some crops—known as cash crops—mainly for sale and export. The nation's most important cash crops include cowpeas, onions, peanuts, and cotton. The local population is the primary consumer of other crops, known as subsistence crops. The main crops of this kind are millet, sorghum (a cereal grain), and rice. Other crops include potatoes, sugarcane, manioc (a starchy root, also called cassava), and vegetables such as tomatoes, cabbage, and lettuce.

INSECT INVADERS

Farmers and herders in Niger faced an additional challenge to their livelihood in 2003 and 2004. These years brought huge swarms of desert locusts. The invasion of these brightly colored insects was the worst in more than ten years. Each adult locust is about 3 inches (7.6 cm) long. It can consume its own body weight in vegetation in one day and may travel as far as 500 miles (805 km) in a single day. An adult female can lay 100 to 150 eggs at time. As massive clouds of these insects descended on Niger, they stripped plants of their leaves, buds, and seeds.

Niger's dry climate and its cycle of droughts present major problems for the nation's farmers. With arable (farmable) land already very limited—making up less than one-fifth of the nation's total area—desertification is also an ongoing concern. Irrigation using the Niger River's water helps add some farmland. The process of creating reliable and efficient irrigation systems is slow and still in progress, however.

In addition to farming crops, raising livestock remains a major occupation in Niger. Herders raise cattle, sheep, goats, and camels.

Desert locusts swarm on a plant stem in western Africa.

A farmer crosses his **millet field** near Maradi. Millet plants grow well in dry areas, but extreme drought and locusts ruin many crops before harvest.

Herders are located mainly in the northern and central parts of the country, and many are still at least seminomadic. In Niger's less arid regions, some herders raise livestock on permanent ranches.

In general, herding families keep some animals and sell the milk that they produce. Other animals are bred and the offspring are sold. Still other herders sell animals for their meat or for their hides (skins), which are made into leather.

For these agricultural workers, drought and desertification are also daunting challenges. They leave less and less vegetation behind for animals to eat. At the same time, continued grazing contributes to further desertification.

The other main areas of agricultural work in Niger are forestry and fishing. In a nation with such limited water resources, neither of these fields makes up a huge portion of the economy. Nevertheless, forestry has grown as some Nigeriens have discovered that the relatively few trees the nation does support can be a very valuable resource. For example, some Nigeriens buy the leaves and bark of certain trees for use in traditional medicines. Seed pods and fruit are also items worth selling. Seeing the trees as a source of continuing income gives Nigeriens a powerful reason to protect them. In addition, with replanting and conservation programs in place, foresters do cut some timber and sell it as fuel and building material.

Hundreds of kinds of fish once swam in the Niger River, and fishing communities have long turned to the river for food and for a source of

A group of men stands in front of the **open-air uranium mine** where they work. One holds a container filled with yellow uranium powder.

income. But the river is suffering as a result of drought and overuse by humans. In modern Niger, fishers have set up fish farms near the river and near Lake Chad. The fish farms reduce dependence on natural fishing and relieve pressure on the strained resources of Niger's waterways. Conservationists hope that fish farms will continue to grow in the future.

Mining and Industry

Mining and industry make up the remaining 13 percent of Niger's annual GDP and employ about 6 percent of the nation's workers. In terms of income, uranium is by far Niger's most important mined material. Uranium is the nation's largest export, and Niger is among the world's top five uranium producers. In recent years, however, drops in uranium prices on the global market have badly hurt Nigerien mining. As prices fall, the costs of extracting the metal from the earth can actually be higher than the profit gained by selling it. Nevertheless, uranium has at times made up more than half of Niger's exports, and the nation hopes to increase production further. But foreign companies dominate the nation's uranium industry, and some Nigeriens have protested that they gain very little from the business.

Coal is another important product of Niger's mines. The nation also produces salt and gold, as it has

NEW CARAVANS AND TRADING POSTS

Niger's uranium exports travel along a path known as the *route de l'uranium*, or "uranium road." The road is about 400 miles (644 km) long and begins at Arlit. This north central town was built in the 1960s specifically for workers at the uranium mines in the region. The uranium road runs from Arlit to Agadez and then Tahoua. There it connects with an older highway.

for centuries. A new gold mine opened in 2004 in northern Niger. Although foreign companies own much of the mine, Niger will also profit if the mine succeeds. Other materials mined in the nation include the metals tungsten, iron, and tin and the minerals gypsum and phosphate.

A newer venture in Nigerien mining is the petroleum (oil) industry. Petroleum, which is used to make gasoline, is believed to exist in northern and eastern Niger. The nation has given several foreign companies permission to look for the resource. So far they have found little, but petroleum could prove valuable if major stores of it are discovered.

Most industry in Niger focuses on processing raw materials. For example, plants in Niger refine sugar, tan leather, and process foods such as peanuts and rice. In addition, Nigerien factories manufacture goods such as cement, chemicals, plastics, soap, and textiles.

Niger imports more goods than it exports to other nations. This gap is called a trade deficit. As this deficit continues year after year, it adds up to major debt.

Transportation and Energy

Niger has an estimated 8,700 miles (14,001 km) of roads, with more planned. Only about 2,250 miles (3,621 km) of them are paved, however. The most important roads are highways linking the nation to its neighbors and connecting its major cities. Niger has no railroad. Air travel is also fairly limited. Niamey has an international airport that operates flights to major western and northern African cities, as well as to Paris, France. In addition, boat traffic can travel up the Niger River during certain parts of the year.

Niger cannot produce enough energy to meet the needs of its people. It produces a very small amount of electricity within its borders. It imports electrical power from Nigeria. Even with this source, electricity outages are relatively common. Some scientists and organizations are working to develop solar energy and other sustainable power sources. In addition, some organizations have worked with rural people to show them how to use donated solar-powered stoves for cooking.

Communications and Media

Many Nigeriens have very limited access to modern means of communication. For example, the nation has an estimated 2 land-line telephone subscriptions for every 1,000 citizens. This rate is among the lowest in the world. Some Nigeriens have cell phones, but these numbers are also relatively small. Computer and Internet use is low, with only about 9,000 personal computers in use in the early 2000s. These figures appear to be growing slowly, especially the number of cell phone users. However, most Nigeriens cannot afford luxuries such as cell phones and computers, particularly in the country's desert and rural areas.

Niger publishes a government-run newspaper, as well as several private papers. While these private papers are technically free to publish what they wish, the government has shut down some publications in the past for being too critical of national politics and policies. Niger's low literacy rate means that radio is a much more popular and important means of receiving news and information. More than 1 million radios are in use around Niger. Listeners can tune into the state-run station, La Voix du Sahel (Voice of the Sahel), which broadcasts from Niamey. The station broadcasts news and other programs in French and several regional languages. Several privately owned stations also exist in Niger. Most also play news and music. In addition, a government-run television channel and a few private channels also broadcast programs. But relatively few Nigeriens have televisions.

BAD BUSINESS

Niger's economy includes a troubling element: human trafficking. Trafficking is the movement of people in order to exploit them in some way, usually by forcing them into labor or prostitution. In Niger, many women and children are trafficked, both from within the country and across borders. Child labor in general is also a problem. Some children are victims of traffickers, while poor families desperate to make ends meet sometimes send their children to work at young ages. The United Nations estimates that up to two-thirds of Nigerien children under the age of fourteen work or beg in the streets. While the government has pledged to crack down on such activities, enforcement is loose and progress has been slow.

The Future

Even as some sectors of its economy grow, Niger remains one of the world's poorest nations. It continues to owe foreign debts that it cannot pay. International aid groups have agreed to help Niger with these debts. The root causes of the debt, however, remain. The primary problem is that Niger lacks the funds and natural resources to export items as valuable and numerous as those that it needs to import. Meanwhile, Niger's people suffer from poor health, little education, and few opportunities.

But Nigeriens have proven time and time again that they can sur-

A truck overloaded with travelers and luggage crosses the desert. Known as **bush taxis,** such vehicles are often the fastest way of reaching remote areas.

vive and even thrive in a harsh environment. Niger's problems will not be easy or quick to solve. Nevertheless, people inside and outside the nation are working to bring more attention to Niger's challenges. Agencies work to end slavery and hunger, increase education and human rights, and boost self-sufficient prosperity. These efforts may soon bring brighter days to this land of contrast and beauty.

Visit www.vgsbooks.com for links to websites with the most current news about Niger's government and economy, including reports on drought relief. Follow links to pages with archived broadcasts from La Voix du Sahel.

CA. 7000–4000 B.C. Ancient residents of the region that will later become Niger carve life-sized images of giraffes into a rock in the Aïr Massif.

CA. 4000 B.C. Cattle-herding settlers live in the area.

A.D. 600S Hausa peoples establish states in eastern Niger.

1000S Tuareg peoples move southward from the Sahara into the Sahel.

1100S Salt is discovered in the Sahara.

1200S–1300S Groups in future Niger begin adopting Islam, which comes to the region through the caravan trade.

1300S The Songhai realm emerges as an important empire. The Tuareg group establishes a realm with Agadez at its center.

LATE 1500S–EARLY 1600S The Kanem-Bornu Empire reaches the peak of its size and influence.

1700S Fulani forces threaten Kanem-Bornu.

1805–1806 The Scottish explorer Mungo Park reaches Niger's region.

1850 German scholar and explorer Heinrich Barth arrives in Agadez.

1899 The Mission Afrique Centrale, led by French military officers Voulet and Chanoinie, reaches Zinder.

1900 France claims the Military Territory of Zinder in the area that later becomes Niger.

1910 France establishes the Military Territory of Niger.

1916 Tuareg soldiers rise up against French forces but are defeated.

1922 Niger officially becomes a French colony.

1926 Niamey becomes Niger's capital under French rule.

1946 France establishes the French Union, making residents of Niger French citizens. The Parti Progrèssiste Nigérien (PPN) forms.

1954 Djibo Bakary leaves the PPN to form the Union Démocratique Nigérienne (UDN).

1956 Djibo Bakary becomes Niamey's first mayor.

1960 Niger wins independence from France. Hamani Diori becomes president.

1960s Uranium mining begins in Niger, centered in the region around the uranium town of Arlit.

1968 A devastating drought hits Niger. Food shortages follow.

1969 Oumarou Ganda's film *Cabascabo* is released and wins international prizes.

1973 A driver crashes into the Tree of Ténéré.

1974 Seyni Kountché leads a military coup that overthrows Hamani Diori. Kountché takes power of the new military government.

1987 Kountché dies and is succeeded by his cousin Ali Saibou.

1989 Nigerien voters participate in the nation's first national elections in almost twenty years.

1990 Student demonstrations erupt in Niamey. A Tuareg rebellion breaks out in the Aïr region, following several years of unrest.

1991 President Ali Saibou holds a national conference to discuss political issues and change.

1992 Nigerien voters approve a new, more democratic constitution.

1993 Mahamane Ousmane is elected through multiparty elections. He becomes the nation's first Hausa president.

1995 Government leaders sign a tentative cease-fire with Tuareg groups to end the rebellion in the north.

1999 During a military coup, President Ibrahim Bare Mainassara is killed by his own presidential guard. Daouda Wanké takes power temporarily. Voters later approve a new constitution and elect Mamadou Tandja president.

2000 Scientists discover the fossilized remains of a large crocodile-like animal in the Ténéré Desert.

2003 Nigerien rap artist Zara Moussa becomes the first female rap musician from West Africa to record an album.

2003–2004 Massive swarms of desert locusts destroy crops and vegetation around the country.

2004 Niger's voters take part in the nation's first local elections. The Samira Hill gold mine opens in northern Niger.

2006 The United Nations sponsors a film workshop in Niamey.

2007 Fighting between the Nigerien army and Tuareg rebels flares up in Agadez.

COUNTRY NAME Republic of Niger

AREA 489,189 square miles (1,266,994 sq. km)

MAIN LANDFORMS Ténéré Desert, Aïr Massif, Djado Plateau, Niger River basin

HIGHEST POINT Mount Bagzane, 6,634 feet (2,022 m) above sea level

LOWEST POINT Niger River, 656 feet (200 m) above sea level

MAJOR RIVERS Niger, Sokoto, Komadugu Yobe

ANIMALS addax antelopes, African puff adders, crocodiles, doves, elephants, fennec foxes, grouse, hycnas, impalas, larks, lions, ravens, sand vipers, warthogs, West African giraffes

CAPITAL CITY Niamey

OTHER MAJOR CITIES Zinder, Maradi, Agadez, Bilma, Djado, Madama

OFFICIAL LANGUAGE French

MONETARY UNIT West African CFA franc. 100 centimes = 1 West African CFA franc.

NIGER CURRENCY

Niger's official currency is the West African CFA franc. CFA stands for "Communauté Financière Africaine," or African Financial Community. Several former French colonies in western Africa use the CFA franc, including Niger's neighbors Mali, Burkina Faso, and Benin. (Several nations to Niger's east and south use the Central African CFA franc.) The West African CFA franc was first created in 1945. It is produced by a central bank in Dakar, Senegal (a nation to Niger's west). Banknotes (bills) are printed in denominations of 10,000, 5,000, 2,000, and 1,000 CFA francs. Coins exist in denominations of 500, 200, 100, 50, 25, 10, 5, and 1 CFA francs. Images on the bills show cultural and rural scenes, as well as regional designs (such as women carrying wicker baskets on their heads) and portraits.

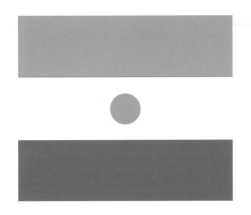

The Nigerien flag was adopted in 1959. The flag is divided into three horizontal bands of color. The top is orange, the bottom is green, and the middle band is white with an orange circle in its center. Multiple interpretations of the flag's colors and symbolism exist. Most observers agree that the orange band at the top represents the desert. However, some believe that the white band symbolizes the Niger River, while others think that it represents purity. Similarly, the orange circle in the middle probably symbolizes the sun, but it may also represent the sacrifices of the Nigerien people. Finally, the green band at the bottom of the flag may stand for Niger's natural resources or it may symbolize hope for the nation's future.

Niger's national anthem is titled "La Nigérienne," or "Song of Niger." It was formally adopted in 1961, one year after independence. The composers Robert Jacquet and Nicolas Abel Francois Frionnet wrote the music, while Maurice Albert Thiriet wrote the words. The anthem is sung in French, but an English translation of the chorus follows below.

Arise! Niger! Arise!
May our fruitful labors
Rejuvenate the heart of this old continent!
And may the song be heard
In the four corners of the Earth
As the cry of a fair and valiant people!
Arise! Niger! Arise!
On the ground and on the wave,
To the sound of the drums
In their growing rhythms
Let us always remain united,
And may each one respond
To this noble future
Which tells us: Go forward!

 Discover what the melody of Niger's national anthem, "La Nigérienne," sounds like. Go to www.vgsbooks.com.

MOUSTAPHA ALASSANE (b. 1942) Born in Niger, Alassane is a director and actor who has made more than twenty-five films. After studying art in Niamey, he met the French filmmaker Jean Rouch and began to focus on filmmaking himself. Alassane also studied and worked in film in Canada before returning to Niger. His first work was *Aouré* (1962), a short nonfiction piece about marriage. In 1965 he made *La Mort de Gandji (The Death of Gandji)*, which is widely thought to be the first animated movie made by a West African director. Alassane eventually became the director of the University of Niamey's film department and continues to make films. In 2007 Alassane was honored with the Légion d'Honneur, a prestigious award given at the Cannes Film Festival in France.

ABDOUSSALAM BA (b. 1939) Born in Niger before the nation's independence, Ba is a physicist. He studied at the Abdou Moumouni University in Niamey and also at the University of Pennsylvania. As a specialist in solar power, Ba has served as the director of Niger's Centre National d'Énergie Solaire (CNES), the National Center of Solar Energy. He has also worked with regional groups in West Africa to promote developing solar energy and other sustainable power sources.

MANO DAYAK (1949–1995) Born in the Aïr Massif region, Mano Dayak was a member of the Tuareg group. He went to high school in Agadez and began learning English from aid workers in the region during the 1960s and 1970s. Dayak later traveled to the United States and went to Indiana University, where he studied folklore. He went on to study political science in Paris, France. While in France, he met his future wife. They married and began a family. They founded a tourism business leading tours through the Aïr and Ténéré regions and to Tuareg villages. Dayak also became a popular and important member of the Tuareg rebellion of the early 1990s. He led one of the many liberation fronts that arose during this period. He also wrote a book discussing Tuareg desires for change in Niger's government. Dayak died in 1995 in a plane crash, while on his way to peace talks with government officials. Many observers—especially among the Tuareg community—believe that the crash was not an accident. They believe that Dayak was killed by his political enemies.

BOULI ALI DIALLO (b. 1948) Born in Niger, Diallo is one of her nation's most prominent educators. As a strong student, she studied biology at Senegal's University of Dakar and in France. She later returned to Niger to work as a biology professor at the Niamey's Abdou Moumouni University. In addition to her science and teaching career, Diallo is involved in programs to improve education in Niger, especially for women. She has served as the country's Minister of National Education and is president of the Forum of African Women Educators. She is also a member of a United Nations education group. She has written and spoken about the need to expand higher education opportunities for Nigerien women.

HAMANI DIORI (1916–1989) Born in Soudouré, a city near Niamey, Diori grew up in a French-controlled Niger. He led a relatively privileged life, as his father worked in the French administration as a public health official. After studying at a teacher training college in Senegal, Diori taught school in Niger for several years in the 1930s. In 1946 he helped found the PPN. That same year, he was elected as a member of the French National Assembly. Following Niger's independence in 1960, Diori became the free nation's first president. He was reelected in 1965 and 1970, but he was accused of corruption. The devastating drought that began in 1968 was the last straw, and in 1974 he was ousted in a military coup. Diori was arrested and imprisoned for six years, followed by another seven years of house arrest. Upon his release in 1987, Diori moved to Morocco, where he died.

ZARA MOUSSA (b. ca. 1980) Born in Niamey, Moussa is a Rap Nigerien musician. In the music world, she often goes by the name ZM rather than using her full name. ZM got her break in 2002, when she won a hip-hop contest in Niamey. Soon afterward she became West Africa's first female rap star to sign a record deal. Her album is called *Kirari*, a Hausa word that was once used to call people to war. ZM's songs address topics such as women's rights, domestic abuse, and other social and political issues.

MAMDOU TANDJA (b. 1938) Born in the city of Diffa, near Lake Chad, Tandja was born to a family with Fulani and Kanuri background. He went to military school in Mali and Senegal. He went on to take part in Seyni Kountché's overthrow of Hamani Diori in 1974 and soon held various position's in Kountché's new government. In 1993 he ran for the office of president himself but lost to Mahamane Ousmane. He tried again in 1996 but was prevented by Ibrahim Bare Mainassara's coup. Finally, in 1999, Tandja won the presidency through democratic elections. He was reelected in 2004.

BOUBE ZOUME (b. 1951) Zoume was born in southwestern Niger into a Songhai-Djerma family who made their living by fishing. He studied administration in Niamey, and he seemed bound for a career in office work. However, he also began writing poetry, and several of his books were published by French companies in Paris. His best known volume of poems is *Les Souffles du Cœur (The Breaths of the Heart)*.

AGADEZ Agadez's location at the edge of the Ténéré Desert draws many visitors who are about to embark on tours across the desert. The town itself also offers interesting sights. One of the best known is its Grande Mosquée, famous for its tall minaret. Visitors can climb the tower's narrow stairs for a dramatic view of the town and the surrounding desert. Agadez also has an old town that holds many interesting houses built in a variety of architectural styles. Like most other Nigerien cities and towns, Agadez is home to several markets, including one that specializes in selling camels, sheep, and other animals.

AÏR AND TÉNÉRÉ NATIONAL NATURE RESERVE This large park boasts some of Niger's most dramatic landscapes, as well as a rich variety of flora and fauna. Among its rarest creatures is the endangered addax antelope. In addition, it is home to more than 350 plant species, 165 kinds of birds, 40 mammal species, and 18 reptile species.

DABOUS ROCK Located about 70 miles (113 km) north of Agadez, this rock bears some of the oldest art in the world. The amazing giraffe engravings here are estimated to be between six thousand and nine thousand years old.

NIAMEY As Niger's capital and largest city, Niamey offers a variety of cultural and historical sights. One of the most important is its Musée National du Niger (National Museum of Niger). Cultural and artistic exhibits highlight important Nigerien handicrafts, ethnic clothing, and traditional weapons. Other sights in Niamey include its *grande marché* (big market). Merchants in the mazelike market sell everything from useful household items such as pots and pans to silver jewelry and vividly dyed cloth. Other sights in Niamey include its large mosque, as well as a Catholic cathedral showing the city's French influences. For sports fans, the local stadium is the place to catch a soccer game.

W NATIONAL PARK Located in Niger's southwestern corner is W Park, one of West Africa's most valuable wildlife preserves. Niger shares the area with Benin and Burkina Faso. The park hosts a wealth of wildlife, some of it rare or endangered. Some of the many mammal inhabitants are hippos, lions, elephants, African buffalo, jackals, and several types of monkeys. More than three hundred bird species populate the skies, and a variety of snakes and other reptiles also call the park home. A vast array of plants also make the park a lush and green habitat for its animals.

ZINDER Zinder's "old town," called Zengou, was once a major stop for merchants in the caravan trade. It is still a place of trade and business and is home to one of Niger's largest markets, held every Thursday. Another part of Zinder, called Birni, holds the dramatic Sultan's Palace. It is still home to a sultan (a regional Muslim leader) and his family, but visitors can take tours of parts of the palace.

animism: a belief system based on the idea that objects have spirits or souls. Natural objects and events such as plants and the weather are all beings and especially important to the faith. In Niger, many people have blended traditional animistic beliefs with ideas from Islam. The resulting blended faith is sometimes called a syncretic religion.

coup d'état: the forceful overthrow or change in government by a small group. Historic coups in Niger have been carried out by members of the army and are called military coups.

desertification: a process in which land is turned into very dry or desertlike land. Niger and other nations in the Sahel region struggle with desertification as the Sahara expands southward.

famine: a severe lack of food, leading to widespread malnutrition and starvation among a population

gross domestic product (GDP): a measure of the total value of goods and services produced within the boundaries of a country in a certain amount of time (usually one year), regardless of the citizenship of the producers

Islam: a religion founded on the Arabian Peninsula in the seventh century A.D. by the prophet Muhammad. The religion's primary tenets are known as the Five Pillars of Islam. Most Nigerien followers of Islam, called Muslims, are members of the Sunni sect, while others follow the smaller Shiite branch of the religion.

massif: a compact group of mountains, especially one that is not connected to other chains or groups of mountains. Niger's Aïr Massif is one of the nation's most dramatic and beautiful landforms.

nomad: a person who travels seasonally or according to the needs of livestock, rather than living in a permanent home year round. Tuareg and Fulani are among the Nigerien ethnic groups who were historically nomadic.

Quran: the holy book of Islam. According to Islamic belief, the Quran's teachings were communicated by Allah (God) to the prophet Muhammad. These divine messages were later collected and recorded in a single volume, which was written in Arabic.

Sahel: a climatic zone in Africa. Not as dry as the desert, the Sahel makes up a large region to the south of the Sahara.

trade deficit: an economic situation in which a nation's imports are of greater value than its exports. Niger has suffered from a trade deficit for many years.

United Nations: an international organization formed at the end of World War II in 1945 to handle global disputes. The United Nations replaced a similar, earlier group known as the League of Nations.

uranium: a metallic element that can be used in nuclear reactors or in nuclear weapons. Niger is among the world's top uranium producers and exporters.

Beckwith, Carol, and Marion von Offelen. *Nomads of Niger.* **New York: H. N. Abrams, 1983.**
This book provides information about the lifestyles and customs of Niger's nomadic ethnic groups. Vivid full-color photos accompany the text.

Conlon, Faith, Ingrid Emerick, and Christina Henry De Tessan, eds. *A Woman Alone: Travel Tales from Around the Globe.* **Seattle: Seal Press, 2001.**
This volume of travel essays includes a story from a woman who traveled to Niger. Part of her trip took her to the Cure Salée, where she witnessed this impressive and colorful gathering of nomadic groups from around Niger and beyond.

Central Intelligence Agency (CIA). "Niger." *The World Factbook.* **2007.** https://www.cia.gov/library/publications/the-world-factbook/geos/ng.html (August 2007).
This CIA website provides facts and figures on Niger's geography, people, government, economy, communications, transportation, military, and more.

Decalo, Samuel. *Historical Dictionary of Niger.* **London: The Scarecrow Press, 1997.**
This thorough source offers detailed information on a variety of places, people, and events in Niger's past. It also offers a timeline, several charts, an overview of Nigerien history, and a lengthy list of sources.

Europa World Yearbook, 2006. **Vol. II. London: Europa Publications, 2006.**
Covering Niger's recent history, economy, and government, this annual publication also provides a wealth of statistics on population, employment, trade, and more.

Finlay, Hugh. *Africa on a Shoestring.* **Berkeley, CA: Lonely Planet Publications, 2001.**
This travel guide provides visitors to Niger with information on lodging, dining, and attractions, as well as offering an overview of the nation's geography, climate, and history.

Geels, Jolijn. *Niger.* **Guilford, CT: Globe Pequot Press, 2006.**
This book is the first English-language travel guide specifically for Niger. Its author discusses the nation's history and provides detailed information on many cities and other places of interest. In addition, she introduces readers and visitors to Niger's culture and traditions, from Rap Nigerien to the appropriate way to greet someone according to local custom.

Naylor, Kim. *Discovery Guide to West Africa: The Niger and Gambia River Route.* **London: Michael Haag, 1989.**
This guidebook gives readers in-depth information on individual cities in Niger, from Agadez to Zinder.

Offodile, Buchi. *The Orphan Girl and Other Stories.* **New York: Interlink Books, 2001.**
This collection of West African folktales includes a Nigerien story about a chameleon who sings and talks to one foolish hunter. Like many traditional stories in Niger and other nations of the region, the story teaches a lesson to those who listen to or read it.

"PRB 2006 World Population Data Sheet." *Population Reference Bureau (PRB).* **2006.**
http://www.prb.org (February 8, 2007).
This annual statistics sheet provides a wealth of data on Niger's population, birth and death rates, fertility rate, infant mortality rate, and other useful demographic information.

Turner, Barry, ed. *The Statesman's Yearbook: The Politics, Cultures, and Economies of the World, 2007.* **New York: Macmillan Press, 2006.**
This resource provides concise information on Niger's history, climate, government, economy, and culture, including relevant statistics.

U.S. Department of State. *Niger: Country Reports on Human Rights Practices.* **2006.**
http://www.state.gov/g/drl/rls/hrrpt/2006/78750.htm (May 19, 2007).
This website is published by the U.S. State Department's Bureau of Democracy, Human Rights, and Labor. It provides a yearly update on the human rights situation within Niger, including concerns about women's rights, slavery, and other issues.

Africa: Explore the Regions: Sahara
http://www.pbs.org/wnet/africa/explore/sahara/sahara_overview.html
and
Africa: Explore the Regions: Sahel
http://www.pbs.org/wnet/africa/explore/sahel/sahel_overview_lo.html
These PBS websites introduce visitors to the people, geography, and environment of the Sahara and Sahel regions of Africa. Listen to a Tuareg wedding song, read a Fulani folktale, hear a camel's call, and more.

BBC News – Africa
http://news.bbc.co.uk/2/hi/africa/
This news site provides a range of up-to-date information and archived articles about Niger and the surrounding region.

CNN.com International
http://edition.cnn.com/WORLD/
Check CNN for current events and breaking news about Niger, as well as a searchable archive of older articles.

Diouf, Sylviane A. *Kings and Queens of Central Africa*. New York: Franklin Watts, 2000.
and
Diouf, Sylviane A. *Kings and Queens of West Africa*. New York: Franklin Watts, 2000.
These books describe the lives and times of some of the major rulers who dominated western and central Africa many years before Niger became a nation.

Di Piazza, Francesca Davis. *Mali in Pictures*. Minneapolis: Lerner Publications Company, 2007.
As Niger's neighbor to the west and as another former French colony, Mali shares many cultural and historical ties with Niger. Read this book to learn more about this West African nation.

Hamilton, Janice. *Nigeria in Pictures*. Minneapolis: Lerner Publications Company, 2003.
This book presents an introduction to Nigeria, Niger's neighbor. Many of the ethnic groups living in Niger, such as the Hausa and Fulani, also live in Nigeria.

Jenkins, Martin. *Deserts*. Minneapolis: Lerner Publications Company, 1996.
This book explores deserts around the world, including the people, plants, and animals who live in these harsh areas.

Lonely Planet: Niger
http://www.lonelyplanet.com/worldguide/destinations/africa/niger/
Visit this website for information about traveling to Niger. You can also see images and learn some background information about the country at this site.

Further Reading and Websites

Nabwire, Constance, and Bertha Vining Montgomery. *Cooking the West African Way.* **Minneapolis: Lerner Publications Company, 2002.**
This cookbook presents a selection of recipes from Niger's region. Cooks in Niger and throughout West Africa use many of the same ingredients and methods to prepare meals.

New York Times Company. *The* **New York Times** *on the Web.*
http://www.nytimes.com
This online version of the newspaper offers current news stories along with an archive of articles on Niger.

SuperCroc
http://www.nationalgeographic.com/supercroc/?fs=www3.nationalgeographic.com
&fs=plasma.nationalgeographic.com
This site from *National Geographic Magazine* offers information about the enormous crocodile-like animal believed to have once lived in the region around Niger. Learn more about the people who found the animal's fossilized remains, see images, and more.

vgsbooks.com
http://www.vgsbooks.com
Visit vgsbooks.com, the home page of the Visual Geography Series®, which is updated regularly. You can get linked to all sorts of useful online information, including geographical, historical, demographic, cultural, and economic websites. The vgsbooks.com site is a great resource for late-breaking news and statistics.

Captions for photos appearing on cover and chapter openers:

Cover: A woman crosses a field of evaporation ponds near Teguidda-n-Tessoumt in western Niger. The ponds are lined with clay, which keeps the salty water from seeping into the ground, taking the valuable salt with it.

pp. 4–5 The city of Agadez, as seen from the minaret (tower) of the Grande Mosquée, sprawls out in a maze of mud-brick homes and businesses.

pp. 8–9 The Ténéré Desert stretches out in front of a lone traveler.

pp. 22–23 Humans inhabiting Niger between six thousand and nine thousand years ago carved animal figures into Dabous Rock in the Aïr Massif.

pp. 38–39 A woman carries two water-filled gourds past granaries containing millet in a Hausa village.

pp. 46–47 The tower of the Agadez mosque rises behind a group of Tuareg camel traders.

pp. 56–57 Seen from above, laborers look like colorful dots amid pools of water at the Teguidda-n-Tessoumt salt factory. Workers mix water with salty earth and then pour the mud into evaporation ponds. As the ponds shrink, the workers scrape crystallized salt from the edges of the pools.

Photo Acknowledgments

The images in this book are used with the permission of: © Holton Collection/SuperStock, pp. 4–5, 11, 13, 36–37; XNR Productions, pp. 6, 10; © Atlantide Phototravel/CORBIS, p. 7; © Frans Lemmens/The Image Bank/ Getty Images, pp. 8–9, 65; Photograph of the Tree of Tenere © Krohn Photos, www.krohn-photos.com, p. 15; © Ken Lucas/Visuals Unlimited, pp. 16, 60; © Nik Wheeler/CORBIS, p. 19; © Roger-Viollet/The Image Works, pp. 20–21; © Silvio Fiore/SuperStock, p. 23; The Art Archive/Biblioteca Nazionale Marciana Venice/Gianni Dagli Orti, p. 25; © CORBIS, p. 26; Adoc-photos/Art Resource, NY, p. 27; © Bettmann/CORBIS, p. 29; © Farrell Grehan/CORBIS, p. 30; © Sébastien Villotte/Sygma/CORBIS, p. 32; © Mary Jelliffe/Art Directors, p. 38; © Tiziana and Gianni Baldizzone/CORBIS, pp. 39, 56; © M. ou Me. Desjeux, Bernard/CORBIS, p. 40; © Djibril Sy/ Panapress/Getty Images, p. 43; © David Rose/Panos Pictures, p. 44; © Issouf Sanogo/AFP/Getty Images, pp. 45, 55; © Warren Jacobs/Art Directors, pp. 46–47; © Images&Stories/Alamy, p. 49; © Victor Englebert, pp. 50, 52; © Todd Strand/Independent Picture Service, p. 53; © Jean Pierre Durand/MAXPPP/ZUMA Press, p. 54; © George Steinmetz/CORBIS, pp. 58–59; © Daniel Berehulak/Getty Images, p. 61; © Olivier Martel/CORBIS, p. 62; © Louise Batalla Duran/Alamy, p. 68.

Front Cover: © George Steinmetz/CORBIS. Back Cover: NASA.